D1264261

THE ISLANDS SERIES

THE ISLES OF SCILLY

THE ISLANDS SERIES

* Published in the United States by Stackpole
† Published in the United States by David & Charles Inc
The series is distributed in Australia by Wren Publishing Pty Ltd, Melbourne

THE ISLES
OF SCILLY

by CRISPIN GILL

DAVID & CHARLES

NEWTON ABBOT   LONDON   NORTH POMFRET (VT)   VANCOUVER

ISBN 0 7153 6957 1

for Molly, who shared and supported all the
early work on this book, but never saw it
finished

Set in 11 on 13pt Monotype Baskerville
and printed in Great Britain
by Latimer Trend & Company Ltd Plymouth
for David & Charles (Holdings) Limited
South Devon House Newton Abbot Devon

Published in the United States of America
by David & Charles Inc
North Pomfret Vermont 05053 USA

Published in Canada
by Douglas David & Charles Limited
132 Philip Avenue North Vancouver BC

CONTENTS

ILLUSTRATIONS

ILLUSTRATIONS

Photographs not acknowledged above are from the collection of Mr F. E. Gibson, whose family has been photographing island life for four generations.

ACKNOWLEDGEMENTS

SCILLY fever caught me when I was sent to the islands as an apprentice reporter to cover the coronation celebrations of King George VI in 1937; no aeroplanes then, no telephones. I took my family back after the war to stay at Parting Carn, on St Mary's, for the first of many holidays. Kathleen and Billy Watts were our first island friends and an endless source of island knowledge; how many friends I have made since, how many holidays spent in various islands, it would be hard to number. My daughter Sarah even worked for a year in the Tresco gardens and flower fields.

So many islanders have helped: Billy and Kathleen Watts, Ronald Watts, W. N. Groves ('Fuzzy'), Tregarthen Mumford (who read the Local Government chapter) and his son Clive, Kenneth Christopher (who read the Farming chapter), John Hamilton, Matt Lethbridge, Frank Gibson, the Clerk to the Council, Mr R. Phillips and his predecessor, Mr R. M. Stephenson, Professor and Mrs L. A. Harvey, and so many more. The late Commander Dorrien Smith made me free of his library at Tresco Abbey and bore my probings patiently; I once interviewed his father. In Cornwall Mr P. L. Hull, the county archivist, Mr H. L. Douch, the curator of the Royal Institution of Cornwall, and my old colleague R. A. Lanyon of Penzance have answered all my questions; above all the late Richard Gillis lent me his collection of *Scillonians* and checked my work on the pilot gigs. In London Mr S. A. Opie, the Librarian to the Duchy, and Mr A. E. Barber, Librarian to the SPCK, made various searches for me, Jo, Countess of Onslow, talked of Agnes, and above all John Pickwell, at his own request, read the manuscript most painstakingly and made many valuable suggestions. I have not accepted them all but I am deeply grateful to him and all who helped. The mistakes remain my own.

Finally, three secretaries have nobly typed the MSS at different times, Mrs M. Emptage, Mrs Susan Shayler and Mrs Peter Carrell, while my wife Betty has patiently borne my long hours at the typewriter and discovered, like the rest of the family, the magic of the isles.

9

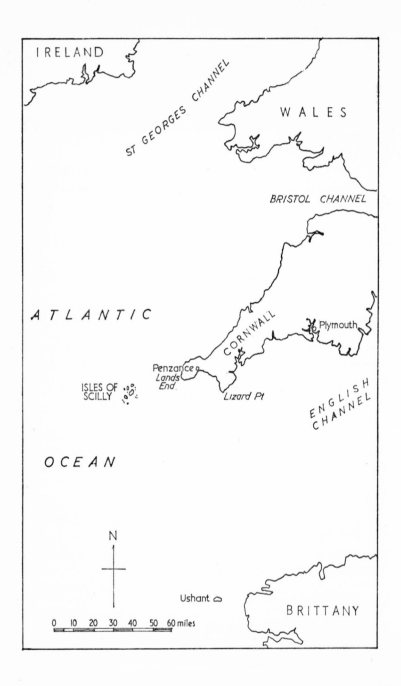

IRELAND

ST GEORGES CHANNEL

WALES

BRISTOL CHANNEL

ATLANTIC

CORNWALL

Plymouth

Penzance
Lands
End.

ISLES OF
SCILLY

Lizard Pt

ENGLISH
CHANNEL

OCEAN

N

Ushant

0 10 20 30 40 50 60 miles

BRITTANY

1   THE EDGE OF THE WORLD

THE Isles of Scilly are the most remote in Great Britain. Just over 2,000 people live on five islands which add up to 4,000 acres, with another fifty-odd islets and uncounted rocks around them. The nearest point of the mainland is Land's End, just over 25 miles from St Martin's Head in the islands. England, Wales and Ireland can show no other islands so remote. In Scotland the Barra group at the southern end of the Outer Hebrides have half the number of people in five times as large an acreage, but they are at the end of a line of islands containing many more people than Scilly. Shetland is much more distant from both Scotland and Norway but has about eight times as many people. Indeed, in all western Europe perhaps only Heligoland can show a smaller community at such a distance from a mainland.

The Isles of Scilly are west-south-west of Land's End. Until the voyage of Columbus in 1492 that was the end not just of England but of the known world. Until 500 years ago, for all men knew, the sea might have been pouring over the edge of the world somewhere west of Scilly. Even the king's judges ventured no further into Cornwall than Launceston, just across the border from Devon. Not until 1716 were they persuaded to penetrate as far as Bodmin, and have got no further west since. No bishop ever made a pastoral visit to the islands until 1832. It is doubtful if any islander had a parliamentary vote before 1832.

These islands have that mystical quality of light that distinguishes the Atlantic seaboard and brought the artists to west Cornwall a century ago. Yet they escape much of the rain, for the figures are low for the West Country and no worse than the English average; they have a sunshine record among the best in Britain and an equable climate in which frost is rare and even a dusting of snow remarkable, winter as balmy as April in London and summer rarely scorching. The commercial flower season is from November to March and gardens flourish all through the year as nowhere else in Britain.

Yet this is no paradise. The flowers only flourish where they can escape the Atlantic gales. Wind velocity figures are among the highest in Britain. Wind-measuring instruments have smashed at 110 miles an hour and seas swept over the top of the 160ft tower of Bishop Rock Lighthouse. On the exposed sides of the islands even gorse will only grow, shaped by the wind, in the shelter of a rock, and the heather lies tight to the thin soil. Yet half a mile away in the lee one can find, even in winter, a sub-tropical garden.

The sea is always master. At matins on St Mary's the chaplain can arrive in oilskins with yachting cap under his arm and apologise: 'I am sorry I am late but boats will be boats. Hymn No 79!' Pillar boxes are cleared 'according to the sailing of the steamer'. Tide tables hang on walls where anywhere else would be bus schedules. Salt-laden gales dictate farming practices. 'God bless Scilly and all who sail in her' is an old joke.

Yet if life is rugged, it is set in beauty, under the high arch of the luminous sky with a sea, clear beyond belief, shading through blues and greens more proper to Greek waters. The islands are like Dartmoor tors set down in this sea but the granite is silver, worn into fantastic shapes by the weather and broken down into sand that makes the beaches almost white, literally glittering with specks of quartz. The best beaches are backed with lush vegetation for they are sheltered from the west; the exposed shores have bare shining rocks running up into gentle downs of thick-carpeting heather.

Tourists now provide the main income but their numbers are limited by the number of beds available. Once the only visitors were those swept off course. In its time Scilly has sheltered Christian hermits escaping the world, outlaws fleeing from England, and pirates glad of its isolation. The leaders of an army defeated in England fled there: it has been seen as a springboard for invasion. It has been a pilotage station and a fishing port; a landfall for mariners struggling in from the Atlantic with food and water exhausted; a graveyard of ships whose crews never saw the fangs of its rocks until too late. Some of its people have sailed to the four corners of the earth in ships built on Scilly beaches. Some never even visited the mainland.

2   IN THE BEGINNING

THE granite of Scilly was formed when the rocks of the Devonian period, laid down upon a seabed between 400 and 350 million years ago, were buckled into a ridge by pressures from the south. Into the hollow domes of this ridge surged molten rock which cooled and hardened into granite. In the 170 million years since that cooling the envelope of sedimentary rock has been worn away to expose granite domes which, still further eroded by weather, form the backbone of the Devon and Cornwall peninsula with the Isles of Scilly as the lowest in height and most westerly of the granite masses. In the long geological process they have at one time been joined to the mainland (though never in human time; there can never have been a lost land of Lyonesse between Scilly and Land's End which man can remember), and at another time under the sea.

The ice ages which began some two million years ago played the last major part in shaping the islands. The ice cap never reached the islands though at its greatest extent the vast glacier coming down between Wales and Ireland had its ice shelf resting on the north coast of the islands, where the 'foreign' pebbles it brought can still be found. The sea level rose and fell with the amount of water held solid in ice; raised beaches, which can be found in most of the islands a few feet higher than the present high-tide mark, show that at one time the islands were roughly of the present shape. Probably at the end of the last glacial period, about 8000 BC, Scilly was one large island. The sea then gradually advanced; when it was 30ft lower than today only the Western Rocks, Annet and Agnes were separated from the rest. That is thought to have been the position about 500 BC; after that the sea made slow inroads with occasional dramatic advances, the last of which seems to have been about AD 370. How shallow the sea still is over the sand flats between St Mary's and the northern islands was demonstrated by John Pickwell of Twickenham in September 1970; in two days and with various companions he made a walk which touched Samson, Bryher, St Martin's and St Mary's.

In the coldest times of the ice ages the soil was frozen right down to the rocks below; in warmer times the half-melted soil slid slowly off the higher ground to deposit brown gravelly layers that geologists call 'head' on the lower levels. Over the centuries sea, wind and rain have worn away the exposed granite, breaking much of it down to sand and working in the weaker 'faults' to chisel even the hardest granite into the massive blocks and weird shapes most dramatically visible at Peninnis on St Mary's. So the islands today are largely made up of granite, head and sand. The wind blows the sand; it has carried it right over the ridge of St Martin's, for instance, and much of Hugh Town is built on a sand ridge linking the Garrison with the main part of St Mary's. The sea still eats into the exposed coasts, threatens from time to time to cut through the sand ridges, moves the sand banks; in modern times the movement of sand is actually building up the size of the islands.

EARLY MAN

The earliest evidence of men in the islands comes from Neolithic stone axe heads, two found on Gugh and one on St Mary's. They were made from the flint pebbles found on Chapel Down, St Martin's (deposited when a river at some point in geological time flowed over the islands south-westwards to cut the valley which is now Broad Sound, the deep-water approach to the islands). Flint is rare in the West Country and was valuable to Stone Age men; this may have been Scilly's first export, about 3000 BC.

A thousand years later comes evidence of men living in the islands, from the tombs of the New Stone Age. These men, the first farmers, had spread northwards from the Mediterranean

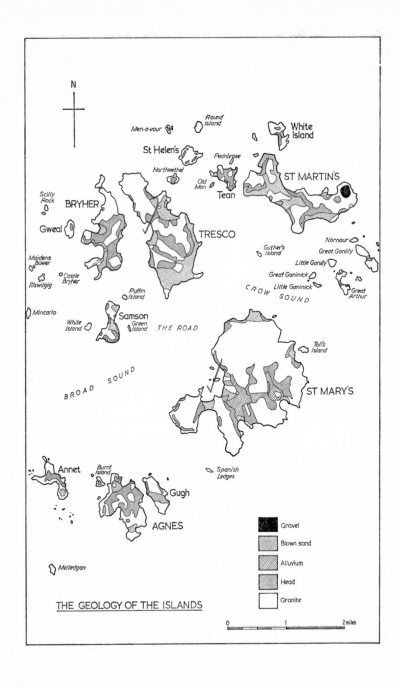

N

Round Island

Men-a-vour

St Helen's

White Island

Pednbrose

ST MARTIN'S

Northwethel

Scilly Rock

BRYHER

Old Man

Tean

Gweal

TRESCO

Maidens Bower

Castle Bryher

Illswilgig

Puffin Island

Mincarlo

Samson

White Island

Green Island

THE ROAD

Guther's Island

Nornour

Great Ganilly

Little Ganilly

Great Ganinick

Little Ganinick

Great Arthur

CROW SOUND

Toll's Island

ST MARY'S

BROAD SOUND

Annet

Burnt Island

Spanish Ledges

Gugh

AGNES

Melledgan

	Gravel
	Blown sand
	Alluvium
	Head
	Granite

THE GEOLOGY OF THE ISLANDS

0   1   2 miles

from about 2000 BC onwards, and those who reached Scilly had followed the sea route, already old, up the coast of Spain and France to Britain's western shores. These Megalithic men are so called because they used megaliths, large stones, with which to build communal burial chambers, reproductions of the caves which their Mediterranean ancestors had used for this purpose. Scilly has over fifty of these tombs, and apart from seventeen in Cornwall and some in southern Ireland there are none like them in Britain. The concentration has led people to write of Scilly as sacred isles where the kings were buried, a dim tradition which culminated in the legend of King Arthur being rowed out to the West from his last battle. But the larger land mass of those days could have supported more people than would the present size of the islands, and they continued to use these graves long after they had gone out of fashion elsewhere. It is believed that Scilly was their first settlement in Britain, from which other colonies were established, and that those who stayed behind, isolated, stuck to the ways of their ancestors. Innisidgen and Bant's Carn on St Mary's may both date back to 2000 BC, but Knackyboy Carn on St Mary's and Obadiah's Barrow on Gugh are probably centuries younger. All were in use for hundreds of years.

But the islands were not entirely isolated. Prehistoric men moved up the west coast of Europe from the Mediterranean and the Biscay shores to Cornwall, Wales, Ireland and Scotland, and faience beads found in Knackyboy Carn are of a type, dated about 1300 BC, found on these routes from Egypt to Scotland. In Knackyboy Carn too were found Middle Bronze Age urns which suggest that these graves were being used after 1000 BC. The burial chamber on Porth Hellick Down on St Mary's, the best preserved in the islands, where one can walk into the now unroofed passage leading into the mound 40ft in diameter and 5ft high, yielded potsherds of the Late Bronze Age. Much play has been made in the past of Scilly being the fabled islands where the Phoenicians came for the tin necessary to make their bronze, but modern geologists doubt if there had been tin in the islands to any extent.

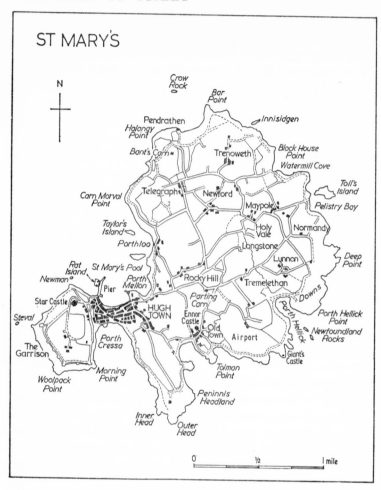

ST MARY'S

Bronze Age houses have been located on St Martin's and low tides reveal on the sand flats from Samson to St Martin's the stone walls that are thought to be the hedges of the corn plots of these early settlers. Early Iron Age pottery was found in the occupation layer on one St Martin's site above Late Bronze Age material, showing continuity of occupation.

Evidence that the Celts reached Scilly in their move across the English Channel comes from Giant's Castle, on the big St

Mary's headland by the airport, where three lines of ditch and earth ramp curve across the neck of the headland. There are similar earthworks on the northern end of Burnt Hill, St Martin's, around the Old Blockhouse, Tresco, and across the northern end of Bryher. The islands were occupied right through Romano-British times; as is demonstrated by the ruins of houses on St Martin's, a grave on Tean where the sea cut into Old Man, and a cemetery of the second century AD found when the council houses overlooking Porth Cressa, St Mary's, were being built. In Tresco Abbey gardens is a Roman altar made of granite, with an axe inscribed on one side and a knife on the other; it is said to have been found in Hugh Town, St Mary's, opposite the Atlantic Hotel. Samson has also yielded a small hoard of Roman silver coins, probably hidden about AD 400.

A Sunday picnic party on Nornour, one of the smallest of the Eastern Isles, made the most interesting discovery of modern times after the spring storms of 1962 had revealed a wall. Excavation over the years since has found a series of rooms with evidence of occupation from Late Megalithic times onwards, and a workshop where small pots and clay figurines were made, as well as bronze Roman jewellery. A pseudo-Venus was the most complete figurine found. Nearly 300 brooches range in date from the middle of the first century AD to just after the end of the second. There is evidence of imported materials, and two studs found probably came from Belgium. The goods were probably made for local consumption, but with the sea level lower than it is today Nornour would have been on the south side of a sheltered little harbour. The Nornour evidence suggests a gradual submergence of the islands, with little activity after the second century BC and a final end after the great submergence of about AD 371.

But continuity of occupation comes from a site some two miles south-west of Nornour, at Halangy Down on St Mary's. Like Nornour, when the sea level was 20ft lower than today it stood on the edge of the now-submerged central area and also close to the seashore, in this case a long arm of the sea reaching up between St Mary's and Tresco. It is believed that the lower huts,

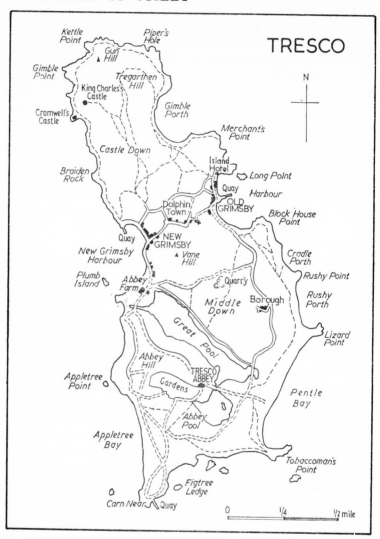

now largely destroyed by the sea, may have been occupied from about 2000 BC by the islands' first farmers, the flint users who buried their dead in Bant's Carn close by, and the other surviving tombs. Soil impoverishment is thought first to have reduced the population and about the third century BC they moved their village up the slope of the hill, as the encroaching sand, which heralded the rising level of the sea, threatened their first homes. By the third century AD their life style had little changed, though some iron was supplementing their flint tools. The houses, originally round, acquired rectangular annexes and show the transition from prehistoric round houses to the shape that has prevailed ever since. Their style of pottery was still in use in Cornwall into the tenth and eleventh centuries, which probably means that this village survived as long, possibly longer. Finally the village was abandoned, perhaps even pulled down, when the occupants may have moved from an increasingly exposed site to the later settlement at Pendrathen.

THE SAINTS

There is other evidence of continuous occupation through the Dark Ages. Built into the priory ruins on Tresco is a stone engraved in the fifth or sixth century AD with Roman capitals, '... THI FILI ... COGVI' – the names cannot be read but 'someone, the son of someone' is remembered. These stones are found through the West Country and west Wales, and are generally connected with the Celtic Christian missionaries from Ireland who sought to keep the faith alive in Britain at this time. To strengthen the Christian idea there are three early graves nearby in the Abbey gardens, covered with slabs of stone and heads to the east; near one was found a stone inscribed with a simple cross.

There are records, as well as the time-magnified legends, which record the movement of Christian preachers and teachers between Ireland, Wales, Cornwall and Brittany in the Dark Ages, as well as records of members of these churches who sought the hermit's life. They sought to follow Christ into the wilderness; and on the western seaboard of Europe the marshes, the lonely places of the coast, and best of all small islands, fulfilled their need. From these hermitages grew the Celtic monasteries.

The ruins of such a hermitage remain on St Helen's. If one creeps a small boat up the cut between the rocks under the eighteenth-century pest house and moves right-handed to the

gentle slopes at the foot of a natural outcrop of granite, a passage-way between stone walls leads to a stone-walled enclosure, buried generally in bracken. Just left of the gateway is a round hut, in the wall itself, like the huts at Halangy Point which can be seen two miles across the sea. The original doorway, hearth and smokehole in the wall behind can be made out; probably it was the cell of the first hermit. In the centre of the enclosure are two rectangular buildings and the higher one, more primitive than the hut, was probably the original oratory. The door on the south side has a cobbled threshold, and the sanctuary at the eastern end is raised with another step up to an altar. Dating of hut and oratory is difficult; they could have been built anywhere between the end of Roman times and the eighth century.

The original hermit and builder, or one of his ancestors, was held in such veneration that a chapel was raised beside his grave, virtually a cleft in the rock. The enclosure wall was built, touching the original hut (and requiring the making of a new doorway) and other huts were built against the wall. These were the cells of the brothers, who were buried in the enclosure. The hermit so honoured is St Ilid. The island was called St Lide's into Tudor times and it was a Flemish mapmaker working for Mercator who altered St Lide into St Helene; his map became the standard chart and the name stuck. Little is known of Ilid. William of Worcester in the fifteenth century said he was the son of a king, and buried on an island in Scilly. The calendar of Tavistock Abbey makes him a bishop, with a feast day on 8 August. ('Saint' merely means an educated man, or a cleric, a Christian trained in a monastic institution.) The earliest settlement resembles others which can be dated to the sixth century, but the only pottery found on St Helen's is tenth-century. It may be that the original hermitage was short-lived but not forgotten, and there was a refoundation in the tenth century.

Other islands had their hermits. Samson was once *Sancti Sampsonis*, and there were ruins, said to be of a chapel, on the sheltered northern side of South Hill which Sir Walter Besant called Holy Hill in *Armorel of Lyonesse*. St Samson, born about AD 480, ranks high among the Celtic saints; he studied at Llanwit in South Wales and founded the great monastery of Dol in Brittany; there is a suggestion (but no evidence) that he once retreated to Scilly for Lent. There were many St Samsons among the Celtic saints, of purely local fame, and the Samson of Scilly may be such a one.

Equally unknown is St Theone, who gave his name to Tean; a papal bull of 1193 refers to *Sancte Theone virginis* and he too may have studied at Llanwit. There is a possible oratory and cemetery on the island, and the rubbish heap near the ruins of

a cottage on Tean goes back to the Dark Ages. St Maugan –
remembered as Mawgan in Wales, Cornwall and Brittany – was
once said to have been Bishop of the Isles of Scilly; an island in
the group was called St Maudud in 1336 and has been identified
as St Martin's. The eastern end is still called Chapel Down,
and an Elizabethan chart shows chapels drawn there, on St
Helen's and Tresco. There was also a hermit of Nurcho, a name
now lost which has been identified as both Norwithel (nearest in
sound but it would be a determined seeker of solitude who
settled there) and Bryher.

All these 'monastic' islands are grouped round Tresco, but as
central government develops in England so their story moves
out of shadows and into documents. Probably it was the giant
Ordulph, earl of Devon and of Cornwall and brother-in-law of

King Ethelred (the Unready), who gave them all to Tavistock Abbey in Devon, which Ordulph's father started and he completed. It seems that the earls of Cornwall already claimed to hold the Isles of Scilly as fiefs. Possibly some monks came down from Tavistock; possibly at this time the chancel of the second church on St Helen's was extended to the east.

THE VIKINGS

But it was not a good time. The Vikings were harrying England from all sides, and about 993 they took Scilly as a base. There is a legend, now discredited, that the leader of the Scilly captors, Olaf Tryggvason, was converted to Christianity by the 'wise man' of St Helen's, and subsequently 'converted' all Norway when he became king. But Scilly was in Viking hands for a time, even as its mother abbey at Tavistock was burnt by the Vikings, and when William the Conqueror came to the throne and had the wealth of England catalogued, the clerks made no mention of the islands in their *Domesday Book*. William's son, Henry I, in 1114 confirmed to the Abbot of Tavistock and to Turold, monk of Scilly, all the islands which had been held by monks or hermits earlier, and the confirmation was supported both by Henry's son Richard, Earl of Cornwall, who named the monastic islands, and the Bishop of Exeter, who named the monastery of St Nicholas. But the Vikings were still abroad; in 1141 three Viking ships south of Ireland 'seized a merchant ship belonging to monks from the Scilly Isles, and plundered it'. In 1155 three Viking chiefs out marauding sailed first to the Hebrides and 'then west to the Scilly Isles, and there won a great victory at Port Saint Mary on Columba's Mass [9 June] and took immense plunder'. The islands were still inhabited but could hardly have yielded 'immense plunder'; perhaps already English merchant ships were anchoring there to wait for the wind. It may have been Vikings who in turn were trapped at Scilly on 8 May 1209, when 112 'pirates' were hanged on Tresco. The islands have their saints; they are not short of pirates and were not to be for some centuries.

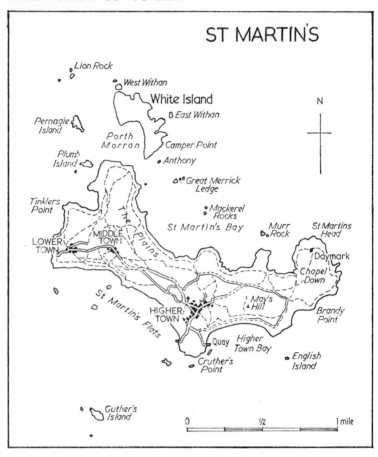

In spite of them the islands developed. In the twelfth century the chapel on St Helen's was extended with a north aisle which brought the founder's grave within its walls. Norman arches which were sketched by Borlase in 1756 pierced the north wall of the old chapel, and an altar of Purbeck marble erected. There are fragments of a similar altar in the priory ruins on Tresco, but the pointed arches that remain there appear to have been built a century later. So much reconstruction has gone into the Tresco ruins that any dating is difficult. There seems no doubt that St Nicholas's Priory on Tresco became the monastic centre but one must not imagine a vast community and great abbey church there; it had but two brothers and never yielded any revenue to the mother abbey of Tavistock.

THE SECULAR ISLANDS

The southern islands were always in secular hands. Agnes is commonly today given a saintly prefix to which it has no right. Its earliest name is Agannas or Haganes, reduced over the centuries to a recognisable Christian name which in turn attracted the saintly prefix. (The only saint on Agnes is St Warna, regarded for centuries by the islanders as a benefactress who brought wrecks. She has the only reputed holy well in the islands, on the edge of St Warna's Cove, open to the fearful Western Rocks and even now rarely free from the debris of the ocean.) St Mary's was originally Ennor. The first mention of a church there comes in 1175, and perhaps because Tavistock Abbey is dedicated to the Virgin Mary, so this church was dedicated to St Mary. The church is older than this mention; there was the Viking victory at 'Port St Mary' 20 years earlier. One rounded arch in Old Town Church may well be twelfth-century, or earlier.

With pirates of all shapes, not just Vikings, ranging the seas, one did not establish conspicuous coastal settlements. The present St Mary's Pool was too open to invaders; Old Town Church sits beside a bay which deep-water ships cannot penetrate, though fishing boats may manage. Beside the little bay the town developed, in the shadow of Ennor Castle. A great natural outcrop of rock at the back of Old Town Bay provides a natural motte for a modest Norman castle; the Lower Moors which still stretch from Old Town Bay to Porth Cressa were wetter and less well drained than today and formed a natural barrier between the castle and any landing in St Mary's Pool. The only land approach to the castle was from the harbourless rest of the island, along the slopes or over the top of Salakee Down. And in the shadow of Ennor Castle grew up the Old Town.

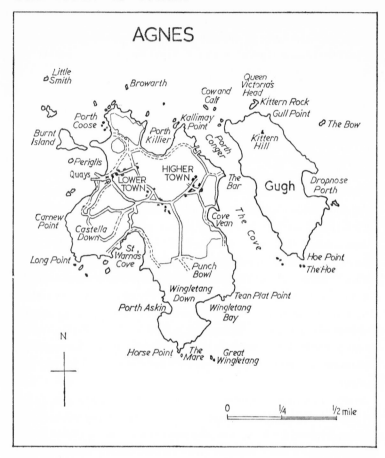

King Henry III appointed Dreux de Barentin, a soldier from the Channel Islands, to be governor of the Isles of Scilly in 1248, with the duty of recruiting a garrison for the castle from among the tenants of Agnes and Ennor. These were the tenants of the Week family, of Week St Mary in north-east Cornwall, who held St Mary's and Agnes by 1150; Richard de Week had to explain in 1195 why he had a chapel at Old Town. His heiress Isabella married Ralph Blanchminster whose father came from Shropshire (Blanchminster, Whitchurch) to Cornwall, possibly attracted by the upsurge in the tin industry.

28

Ralph made religious foundations in Bodmin and acquired Caerhays in Roseland. Their son Ralph became lord of Caerhays, Week St Mary, Stratton and Scilly; the remains of his great house at Bien Amie near Bude is now part of Binhamy Farm and a trust he set up still owns much of Bude. In 1270 Ralph went on the Fifth Crusade with Prince Edward, and when that prince became King Edward I in 1272 he made Blanchminster constable of Ennor on condition that he found twelve men-at-arms to serve there. Ralph's son died before his father, and he was succeeded by his young grandson, another Ralph. The boy's mother married again and in 1301 his step-father, John de Allet, was his chief tenant in the islands. In that year both the Abbot of Tavistock and Blanchminster in their respective islands established their claim to the assize of bread and ale (which meant control of trade) and to all wrecks, excepting all gold, whale, scarlet cloth and fir or masts, which were reserved to the king. This right to anything cast up by the sea is not peculiar to Scilly; it crops up in most coastal properties of the day and was of great value in Cornwall.

Blanchminster's tenants in 1301 were listed as John de Allet, William le Poer, and Philip de Allet. Poer was also the king's coroner in the islands and in 1305 he ran into trouble of a kind which illustrates the character of the islands. He had gone to Tresco to investigate a wreck and take charge of its cargo, but he was seized by a mob led by the prior. The men-at-arms and their captain from Ennor Castle were with the prior, and Poer was flung into the prison of La Val and kept there until he had paid a fine of 100s. The complaint he sent to the king said that Blanchminster was failing to keep peace in the islands by allowing in felons, thieves, outlaws, and men guilty of manslaughter.

When the only surviving records are those of crimes it is difficult to judge a community, but we must read this story against the background of a man from St Levan killing a Sennen man in the islands in 1284 (it was declared a fair fight), of Thomas Richiou murdering a monk on Tresco in 1302, of women charged with theft being marooned on Bishop Rock with a couple of loaves and a pitcher of water, and left to drown, of a clerk (which means a man of the church) being sent to prison on the mainland for theft. Even Poer was accused of stealing a whale, which was of course a 'wreck' reserved for the king. Blanchminster was not held seriously to blame for the lawlessness; he was one of the two members of Parliament for the county in 1314 and in that year received licence to embattle Ennor. (The only other defended place in Cornwall was St Michael's Mount.) When the Black Prince was made duke of Cornwall in 1337 the Isles of Scilly were listed under the 'foreign rents' of the Duchy. Blanchminster paid 300 puffins or half a mark; a century later the rent was down to 50 puffins or 6s 8d. With the creation of the Duchy, Blanchminster released his keepership of Ennor, and all his island rights, to his cousin John de Allet.

WAR, PESTILENCE AND PIRATES

It was not a profitable move for Allet; the Hundred Years War with France had just started. In 1342 a force of 600 Welsh archers on their way to Brittany were in the islands for 20 days, no doubt storm-bound. Whatever other trouble they caused in that time, when they went they took everything portable and eatable, leaving only two ploughing oxen on St Mary's. They were accused of having carried off £500 of crops. So at least the islanders said a little later, in excuse for not paying dues. Five years later the islands were only worth £18 a year. Then came the Black Death. In 1348 the rents were low 'because the great part of the fishermen have died this year by the pestilence'. Old Blanchminster had died and the Duchy was guardian of his heir, his grandson John. The Duchy returns for 1348–9 record, apart from the plague, that there were no rents for the 'taberna vini' (is this the wine shop?) or the windmill, because both had been destroyed 'by the foreigner'. Clearly island life had been developing before the war, in spite of the lawlessness. In 1352 the constable, Walter Hull, was ordered to apprehend some bondmen that had fled to the islands from Cornwall; they were still a refuge for outlaws as well as pirates. It was at this time that the Abbot of Tavistock, who had a year or so before withdrawn his monks from Tresco, leaving the islands in the hands of secular ministers, declared that the priory in Scilly was nearly bankrupt because of various misfortunes, including the Black Death and the devastation of the islands by pirates.

Edward III made an appeal in 1367 to all lords, admirals, soldiers, sailors, and so forth, that they should guard St Nicholas's Priory, because for want of proper protection it was wasted and impoverished by the frequent arrival of ships of all nations '. . . *in tantum destructus et depauperatus existat* . . .'. The bishop removed a weak prior and substituted a stranger in Richard Auncel, who became prior of St Michael's Mount in 1381 and during his active sojourn there built the quay at Mousehole, across the bay, Cornwall's first artificial harbour. Not until 1442 is another prior of Scilly mentioned, Hugh Denyngton, when he received a commission to punish all crimes and excesses in the islands. Only adultery and incest were specified, sins not surprising in an isolated community. Denyngton reached high office, becoming Abbot of Tavistock in 1451, and was given the privileges of a bishop by the pope. No doubt it was on his intercession in 1461 that the pope excommunicated all pirates who raided Scilly, and offered indulgences to penitents who went to the shrine of St Elidius (on St Helen's) and contributed to its repair. Whoever drew up the document knew his islands, for he could say that the shrine was well visited. But the pirates, excommunicated or not, were winning. Later records of Tavistock Abbey say no more about their possessions in the islands. When the abbey's possessions and income was recorded by the king's commissioners before Henry VIII dissolved the monasteries, not a word referred to Scilly. Most of Tavistock Abbey's land went to John Russell, who became Lord Bedford. It is all carefully listed, but again Scilly is not mentioned. Either the abbey had abandoned the islands or they were worthless.

The civil ownership tells a similar story. John Blanchminster died without issue in 1373 and his estate reverted to his younger brother Guy, rector of Lansallos. He of course was childless and the eventual heir was their sister's daughter, Emma. Her first husband, Sir Robert Tresillian, chief justice to King Richard II, was executed in 1399, when Henry IV came to the throne, and she then married Sir John Coleshill. Guy Blanchminster made over all his lands to them. Their son was killed at Agincourt in 1415 and the land passed to a minor; on his death it was taken by an heiress to Sir Ramfrye Arundell. Their daughter, Elizabeth, was their heir and she was married first to a Whittington of Gloucestershire and then to a man called Stradling. A daughter of the second marriage married a Danvers of Wiltshire, and the islands were sold to Thomas Lord Seymour. He had not bought very much – an inquiry in 1484 declared that the islands in time of peace were worth 40 shillings, and in time of war nothing.

Leland described the islands in 1542, though he may have got no nearer than the Land's End. He calls St Mary's 'a poore Toun and a meately strong Pile, but the Roues of the Building in it be sore defacid and woren'. It is not clear whether it was the dwellings of the town or the castle that were ruinous. Iniscaw ('sum caulle this Trescauw') belonged to Tavistock Abbey and there 'was' (note the past tense) a poor cell of monks there. It had a little fortress and a parish church that a Tavistock monk served in peacetime. There were about sixty households. Agnes 'so caullid of a Chapel theryn' was deserted, almost all of the five households that had lived there having gone to a wedding or a feast on St Mary's, and been drowned when going home. It is a story that constantly crops up in island history. Rat Island (Samson?) had so many rats that they would devour a horse or any other living creature that went ashore there. Bovy Isle (Bryher?) and St Martin's are just mentioned; there were wild boars on 'Innissehawe' and on St Lide's island 'yn tymes past at her sepulchre was great superstition'. Note again the past tense. In many of the islands the ruins of houses could be seen. 'Few men be glad to inhabite these islettes for al their plenty, for robbers by the sea that take their catail of force. These robbers be French men and Spaniardes.'

So the saints had gone, and the pirates had taken over. Piracy

Page 33   The two sides of Bryher on the same winter's day: (*above*) the west coast with its bare granite rocks only protected from the Atlantic by the off-lying rocks and (*below*) Bryher Town on the eastern shore, looking down over the high hedges of the flower fields to the boats laid up on the sand. Note the gig *Czar*, built about 1874

Page 34 Two aerial views: (*above*) looking across St Mary's to Hugh Town on its narrow isthmus with Garrison beyond and the Quay on the right hand; (*below*) the 1680 lighthouse on Agnes in the middle of the flower fields, with the sand bar linking Gugh to Agnes in the right background and St Mary's beyond

was the scourge of the Channel right through medieval times; when central government was weak the English pirates operated out of ports like Plymouth and Fowey, indeed most ports, where they openly sold their prizes. When central government was strong and kept naval forces at sea, then the worst of the pirates retreated to lonely places like the Irish coast, Milford Haven, and the Isles of Scilly. It was not a pirate's lair like the Tortugas in the West Indies in the seventeenth century; Scilly was too far from the trade routes. But pirates of all nations retreated there to lick their wounds; enemy ships from France and Spain could move into the roads in wartime and the population could not say them nay. One might almost say that many of the inhabitants, or at least their ancestors, were people who had made England too hot to hold them.

These were the islands that Thomas Seymour bought in 1547. His brother, the Duke of Somerset, was Protector to the infant King Edward VI but Thomas Seymour had married Henry VIII's widow Catherine Parr and plotted to take over the country. He collected arms, used his position as admiral to go half-shares with the pirates of the Bristol Channel and finally, when his wife died, aspired to marry Princess Elizabeth. When a Bill of Attainder was brought against him in 1549 he was accused of entering into relations with pirates, 'to have gotten into his hande the strong and dangerous isles of Scilly where he might have a safe refuge if anything for his demerits should be attempted against him'. With his execution the islands of St Mary's and Agnes fell to the Crown. The other islands had passed to the Crown with the dissolution of the monasteries, and it was decided that Scilly would never be a threat to England again. But no wonder that the new man who came in, Godolphin, could look back and say that Scilly had been nothing but 'a bushment of briars and a refuge for all the pirates that ranged'.

3   DEFENCE

TUDOR CASTLES

THE Isles of Scilly assumed a new importance for England after Columbus had crossed the Atlantic in 1492; from being on the edge of the known world they became a milestone to the new world. But not until Henry VIII had broken with Rome, and it was necessary to guard against any attempt by the Catholic kings of France and Spain to restore the Pope's authority in England, was any attempt made to defend the isles. About 1540 Henry built a castle on the high ground in the north of Tresco, looking down on the entrance to New Grimsby harbour. Guns of course were still novelties; some 10 years later it was found that these high embrasures did not really command the harbour and a new round tower to hold guns was built below, at water level. Perhaps it is typical of Scilly that the castle is now called King Charles's Castle and the fort below Cromwell's Castle. Both survive in remarkable condition, commanding the most beautiful views.

It was to inspect these defences early in the reign of the boy king Edward VI that Lord Admiral Seymour sailed from St Michael's Mount in 1547. This visit may have shown him the potential of the islands as a base for his attempt on the throne of England, and after his execution in 1549 more reliable guardians were appointed. William Godolphin, son of a leading figure in Cornwall, and John Killigrew, governor of Pendennis Castle at Falmouth, were commissioned to survey the islands, after which Killigrew was instructed to 'make the fort in our lady's isle at Scilly . . .' He spent £6,000 of royal money and installed a garrison of 150 men on St Mary's and Tresco, but what was built is now uncertain. The dashing ambitious Killi-

36

grews were notoriously extravagant, amassing debts as well as distinction and not above consorting from Falmouth with the pirates of the Helford River. This last link threw Killigrew and his son into prison and cost them Pendennis.

Against this Godolphins pursued the path of virtue. Sir William was thanked by the Privy Council in 1556 for apprehending the pirate Jacob Tompson and his three ships in the islands. His son, Sir Francis, became the leading man in Cornwall after Sir Richard Grenville moved into national affairs, and in 1570 he took a lease of all the Isles of Scilly. He drew guns and ammunition from the Tower of London – the nation's armoury – for the defences of the islands, and was authorised to recruit his tenants in the isles as a garrison in time of war, and to draw provisions for them from Cornwall.

A picture of Scilly at this time is provided by a map in the Cotton Collection in the British Museum, believed to have been drawn by the Dartmouth navigator John Davis in 1585. His ships were anchored off New Grimsby, protected by the castle. Two batteries on St Mary's covered Watermill Cove, where he watered his ships, and the eastern entrance to Crow Sound. There is a house on Telegraph – later called the Watch-house – but the only group of houses is at Old Town, flanked by the Castle of Ennor and Old Town Church.

The Spanish planned to use Scilly as a rendezvous for their Armada in 1588 and some ships did reach the islands. In 1590 Spain was establishing a naval base in Brittany and more active steps were taken to defend the islands. Godolphin in 1593 was commissioned to build a fort on St Mary's. Robert Adam, a Crown officer, was the engineer; at the same time he was building a fort on Plymouth Hoe and rebuilding Pendennis at Falmouth, clearly regarded as the three keys to the West. His work, Star Castle, still dominates St Mary's Pool, a most romantic survival in the shape of an eight-pointed star, little changed over the years and with the date 1593 over the doorway. It was not actually finished until December 1594, just in time. Four Spanish galleys from Brittany landed troops in Mount's Bay the following summer who burnt the villages round the bay before Godolphin drove them back into their boats. Built at the same time probably was another fort on the other side of St Mary's Pool; it is uncertain that it was ever completed and to add to the confusion the substantial ruins are now called Harry's Walls. The Old Blockhouse on Tresco, commanding Old Grimsby harbour, and a much more satisfactory ruin, is of this date. Star Castle was made secure by a wall with gun emplacements being built across the narrow neck of land to protect the Hugh, on which the castle stands. Any attacking soldiers would have had to advance across the narrow neck of sand on which Hugh Town now stands; the whole Hugh became a fort and has been called the Garrison ever since. In 1603 the first pier was built in St Mary's Pool; it is still in use as the inner pier of the harbour.

THE CIVIL WAR

The Stuart kings neglected the island defences, save for a brief spending spree when Charles I went to war with Spain in 1625. Even this did not stop many islanders scuttling to the mainland in 1628 for fear of a Spanish occupation. The islands seem wide open. The pirate William Harvey sold his Mediterranean plunder on Tresco in 1603, and a crew of Barbary pirates, the scourge of the Channel in the early seventeenth century, is said to have passed a whole summer on Great Ganilly after being wrecked in the Eastern Isles.

The Godolphins, still leading figures in Cornwall, declared for the King when Civil War came. The islands were left undisturbed until the very end. Then young Prince Charles, who had been sent to the West nominally in command with a group of privy councillors to advise him, but really for his safety, moved under pressure by Fairfax and Cromwell from Bristol to Launceston to Falmouth and finally to the Isles of Scilly. He took ship in the *Phoenix* from Sennen on 2 March 1646 when Fairfax was at Bodmin. With the fourteen-year-old Prince were his advisers, led by the Earl of Clarendon, gentlemen of Cornwall, and a group of Royalist refugees, who, in spite of their titles, found little comfort. They embarked at midnight, were very sick on the crossing, and even pillaged by the crew.

So Scilly received one of its first royal visitors. He was housed with his staff in Star Castle and the black oaken chair which served as his royal seat is now used by the chairman of the Council of the Isles of Scilly at formal meetings. Charles must have been cramped in the castle, but the refugees fared even worse in the cottages clustering at the foot of Garrison Hill, the beginnings of Hugh Town. There was little food or fuel in the islands to sustain this influx of 300 gentle people, far more than the island's normal population, and what little came from France was bad. All Cornwall was falling to the Parliamentary forces, whose ships were off Scilly, and after six weeks the whole party of Royalists sailed for Jersey in the *Proud Black Eagle*, arriving there on 16 April. On 25 August Parliamentary troops occupied Scilly. Francis Godolphin had gone with the Prince to Jersey; though he returned to Cornwall during the Commonwealth he was closely watched and once arrested.

The islanders rapidly grew to dislike the Roundhead garrison, largely because they were not paid for billeting them. The troops found their pay falling months behind. In the second Civil War of 1648 the Cornish rebels were soon crushed but one Sunday morning in September when the Governor of Scilly, Colonel Anthony Buller, and his officers were at church, the garrison mutinied and declared for the Royalists. The islanders did not object and Sir John Grenville, whose father had died fighting for the king and whose great-grandfather was Grenville of the *Revenge*, was sent to turn the islands into a base for the Royalist privateers. He arrived as governor on 22 February 1649; King Charles had been executed three weeks before and Grenville's first act in Scilly was to proclaim the young Prince of Wales as King Charles II of England. Lord Hopton, the old Royalist commander in Cornwall, brought in twenty ships and made himself a menace to Commonwealth naval craft and merchantmen. In April he fought a battle against a merchant fleet in which 100 sailors were killed and the ships taken to Scilly. Plymouth and Pendennis were reinforced against this Scillonian threat, Cornwall with its Royalist sympathies carefully watched, and one writer called Scilly 'a second Algiers' – the headquarters of the Barbary pirates.

The line between privateers and pirates is always thin, and the Scilly ships began attacking Dutch as well as English ships. Holland, the old ally against Spain, had taken much of England's carrying trade at sea during the Civil War and a base in Scilly would have been invaluable to the Dutch. With the excuse afforded by Grenville's privateers Admiral Van Tromp appeared with a dozen ships early in 1651. He invited Sir John Grenville to hand the islands over to him, to keep safe for Charles II. Grenville refused; he was still an Englishman. While Tromp was still off the islands Robert Blake appeared with an English fleet. Tromp offered to help him reduce the islands, but Blake most tactfully declined.

During their three-year occupation the Royalists had considerably strengthened the islands, with earthworks on St Mary's covering the Crow Sound approach all the way from Toll's Island to Carn Morval. The battery on Toll's Island can still stir the imagination but that at Bar Point, largely made of sand, is now a shapeless mass. Another earthwork had been built at the tip of Peninnis and probably a breastwork all round the Garrison. On Tresco the Tudor stone castle was improved (and given its modern name of King Charles's Castle) while earthworks were also erected on the southern tips of Tresco and Bryher to cover St Mary's Pool. With about 1,500 defenders, St Mary's would be a hard nut to crack.

Blake did not attempt it. He is reputed to have taken his ships in through the rocks on the northern side of the islands and anchored in St Helen's Pool, out of range of the Blockhouse at Old Grimsby. Others argue that he hove-to north of Round Island, but wherever the ships were, the soldiers were sent in to attack from boats. After an initial mistake in landing his soldiers at Norwethel, Blake got his men ashore on Tresco. King Charles's Castle, menaced from the landward side, was no longer tenable and on 12 April the Royalists abandoned it and retired to St Mary's. Island legend says that before moving out they blew up the castle. Over the years the blown sand filled the ruins until the tops of a few walls alone were visible until the site was excavated in the early 1950s and most of the ground-floor walls found standing but choked with the debris of the first floor. This might bear out the explosion legend. With Tresco in his hands Blake could now use New Grimsby harbour. He built a new battery at Carn Near at the southern end of Tresco, a little higher than the Royalist battery – it is still there, on top of a rocky knoll and still called Oliver's Battery – from which St Mary's Pool could be brought under fire. With these guns, and with his ships cutting off supplies from Jersey and France, Blake sat down to starve out Grenville and his men. At the end of a month the Cavaliers accepted his honourable terms; a convoy home for the Irish soldiery and to France to join the King for the Englishmen.

King Charles's Castle was left in ruins but the waterside tower was improved; from these works it takes its modern name of Cromwell's Castle. Parliament put a garrison into the island but left them short of supplies. With the Restoration of Charles II in 1660, Sir Francis Godolphin, grandson of the man who built Star Castle, resumed the family lease and the title of Governor. The Dutch were still a menace; a month or two after their fleet had sailed into the Medway in 1667, some of their ships appeared off Scilly. The Dutchmen landed on some of the off-islands and stole some sheep, and Star Castle fired on their boats when they came within range.

THE INVALIDS

With the end of the Dutch wars the number of troops was much reduced. After the creation of Chelsea Hospital in 1688 companies of invalids were formed from its pensioners and used as garrison troops. Such a company, about two dozen strong, formed the military might of Scilly for most of the eighteenth century and the uniform the Chelsea Pensioners still wear must have been a familiar sight in Hugh Town. They were billeted in the town and probably rarely climbed the hill to the Garrison.

Two or three were detached to Tresco, and another small party formed a look-out on St Martin's, where they had a small guardhouse above Higher Town. A 1765 report said all the men were unfit for service because of 'the infirmities of old age, and crazy constitutions'.

The governor was rarely if ever in the islands. The senior soldier was lieutenant-governor, but he often preferred to live in Penzance and leave the command to a junior officer. One military man who seems to have become a real islander was Abraham Tovey, sent down in the early 1740s to improve the island defences. He was given the White House, still on the northern tip of Garrison and overlooking St Mary's Pool, as a reward for his bravery as an artillery officer in the War of the Austrian Succession. He was master gunner, store-keeper, barracks-master, and collector of the lights. On Tresco he built a platform for a battery of guns on the seaward side of Cromwell's Castle. On St Mary's he strengthened and largely rebuilt the wall around Garrison, and the gate through which one approaches Star Castle is his work. Under the simple bell embrasure is the royal monogram and the date 1742, and below that, in even larger letters than those of the king's initials, his own 'A.T.'. Around Garrison he not only set up the eighteen batteries complete with big guns, but also cut a road which enabled all the batteries to be served and still makes a splendid promenade, long renowned as a sunset walk.

THE NAPOLEONIC WARS

Under threat of war, as in 1757 and 1763, the Garrison was strengthened. Scilly was defended by twenty-four Invalids when the French Revolutionary Wars broke out in 1794, but the new commandant was authorised to form a Corps of Land Fencibles (the Home Guard of the day) just over 100 strong, armed and equipped by the government. The men of Scilly promptly enlisted, drew their 4 guineas levy money, set up a watch at Mount Todden, attended two parades a week and were free from the dangers of the press gangs. These had pursued the island men and raided merchantmen anchored off Scilly right through the eighteenth century. By 1798 more regular soldiers had reinforced the garrison, and the Fencibles were disbanded.

After the short Peace of Amiens, Sea Fencibles were embodied in the six inhabited islands with freedom from press gangs again and a shilling attendance pay for each of four drills a month. The drill ground of the St Mary's contingent was on the outskirts of Hugh Town as it then was; now houses enclose it and a public park made about 1890, but it is still called 'The Parade'. These Fencibles were disbanded after Trafalgar but the garrison commander, not trusting the strength of the Navy alone, built three Corsican (or Martello) towers, 20ft high with a 32-pounder carronade on top, at Telegraph, on Buzza Hill east of Porth Cressa, and on Garrison. They still stand.

The naval squadron blockading Brest and the frigates 'patrolling to the westward' used the island anchorages from time to time. The daymark on St Martin's was a signal station, and the ruins of the houses built for the look-outs can still be seen nearby. A signal from St Martin's one day told Sir Edward Pellew, anchored with his frigates, that a French ship was in sight. He gave chase, captured her, and found two Agnes fishermen aboard. Not recognising her as French they had offered their services as pilots and been taken prisoner. Another legend tells of a French barque becalmed off Broad Sound. Nineteen men from Samson captured her, and were all drowned sailing her to the prize court at Plymouth.

From time to time convoys of merchantmen were assembled at Scilly, and a surveyor-general of the Duchy put up a scheme for turning the islands into a harbour of refuge, with a breakwater from Samson to Agnes, and another from Agnes out to the Spanish Ledges. Nothing ever came of the plan, but seeing how uncomfortable an anchorage can be in the harbours of refuge that were built (it was a fashionable idea at the time) it may be just as well.

NINETEENTH CENTURY

So too did the Invalids fade away. Among the last commandants was Lieutenant-Colonel George Vigoureux, remembered in Quiller-Couch's novel *Major Vigoureux* as a placid, whist-playing old man. In 1822 the garrison consisted of a lieutenant-governor, a master gunner, four gunners and two or three aged sergeants; in 1857 five Invalids; and by 1863 one elderly caretaker alone supervised the defences. With the final disbandment of the garrison in 1863 all but two of the fifty 32-pounder guns in the Woolpack battery were removed. There is a story that the 32-pounders in the Garrison came from HMS *Colossus* after she was wrecked on Southern Wells, south of Samson, in December 1798. When the remaining guns were repaired in 1968 it was thought that they had been made at Woolwich Arsenal between 1790 and 1820.

Between 1896 and 1902 Scilly was re-armed. New emplacements were built in Garrison, one overlooking Woolpack and the other at the next point north, overlooking Steval. Another battery was set up at Bant's Carn. The War Department steamer *Lord Wolseley* brought in four 6in guns and a company of the Royal Garrison Artillery spent three weeks getting the guns in place. At one time it looked as if old Abraham Tovey's archway over the Garrison entrance would have to be taken down, but the problem was solved by lowering the road. Then in 1904 the Duke of Connaught, newly appointed Inspector-General of the Forces, came down. He condemned the 6in guns because all the navies of the world were using 8in guns, and very soon guns and soldiers were packed up and off again.

WORLD WAR I

With the outbreak of war in 1914 Scilly found itself on the edge of the battlefield. The start was signalled on 5 August 1914 when the cruisers *Doris* and *Iris* brought in two German sailing ships. The following spring the islanders had a dramatic introduction to submarine warfare, when the *U29* set the *Indian City* on fire to the south of St Mary's. Watching crowds on the hilltops, attracted by the great pillar of smoke, saw the U-boat towing the ship's lifeboats towards the island until the tiny patrol boats from St Mary's Pool steamed out, blazing away with their little guns. *U29* dropped the two boats and made off on the surface towards the steamer *Headlands* which had appeared over the horizon. The *Headlands* was torpedoed and sunk, and then, 25 miles to the west, *U29* met the Ellerman liner *Andalusian*, boarded her and opened the valves after ordering the crew away. The mail boat *Lyonnesse* and other small Scilly craft tried to tow the *Andalusian* in, but she went down.

It was the start of a long saga. Over fifty vessels were lost to U-boats in or near Scilly waters to the certain knowledge of the islanders. Sometimes broken up and battered ships crept into the roads to be patched up; sometimes lifeboats, often days at sea, came up on the island beaches or were found by the patrol boats. The rescued seamen were of all nationalities. Coastal patrols were set up in the islands and all sorts of alarms of U-boats being seen close in, or stalking ships at anchor in the roads, were rife. Bryher men once reported seeing the *U34*, which was hovering about in June 1915, close in to the rocks disguised as a sailing ship. In February 1917 the Agnes lifeboat saved forty-seven men from seven Dutch ships and one Norwegian, torpedoed in a neutral convoy off Bishop. In September 1918 the White Star liner *Persic*, which had been torpedoed in convoy 50 miles west of Scilly while carrying 2,108 American soldiers, was brought in, waterlogged and listing, to anchor in the roads for repairs. The soldiers were all taken on to Plymouth but the white bread baked for them was sent ashore, with biscuits and joints of frozen meat, a godsend to the rationed islanders on dark sawdusty wartime loaves. In January 1918 the destroyer *Furious* struck the Crim Rocks, just north of the Bishop, in fog, but was towed in by the tug *Blazer* and berthed alongside St Mary's Quay, the first and last destroyer ever to come alongside there. *Blazer* herself was the last casualty of the war, wrecked on Armistice night 1918 just north of Woolpack, but all twenty-eight aboard her were saved.

45

The island population swelled by about 1,000 men during the war. About 700 men were attached to the naval sub-base on St Mary's. The officers were in the White House, Tovey's old residence; Tregarthen's Hotel was the wardroom, Holgate's the sick bay, the Church Hall an army and navy club. Wrens served as typists at the White House or attendants at Tregarthen's. Trawlers, drifters and tugs were based in St Mary's Pool, with workshops on Rat Island. Q-ships, the small coasters with hidden guns sent out to trap U-boats, always excited comment when they appeared. The piers, Garrison, and the wireless station at Telegraph were guarded by forty or fifty soldiers – at one time convalescent men of the 3rd Devons. There were a few Royal Marines, and local volunteers were trained for service in any emergency.

Yet the biggest change brought to the islands came in February 1917, when Curtiss H 12 'Large America' flying boats were sent down from Plymouth to start an air base in the islands. It was planned to set up the base at Porth Mellon, on the eastern side of St Mary's Pool, but when nearly completed it was ruled out as unsuitable and the base moved to Tresco. The slipway, the concrete flats on which the planes were parked, and some of the wartime buildings are still there, used by the Abbey farm on the shore just south of New Grimsby. Short 184 seaplanes were added, and for the rest of the war flew anti-submarine patrols over the convoys passing close to the islands. The station grew to twenty-two aircraft. In August 1918 a new squadron, No 234, was based on Tresco, with Short 225 seaplanes. A number of U-boats were sighted and attacked, and among those claimed sunk from the air was the one which crippled the *Persic*. The great value of the planes was that their presence in the air meant that submarines had to stay deep to avoid being seen. It was a rugged and exposed base for primitive aircraft, and a number were lost. Eight officers from the base died on operations, and a bomb explosion on Tresco killed several men.

WORLD WAR II

War came again to the islands on 3 September 1939 as it did to most communities, with gas masks being issued and an air-raid siren on top of Hugh Town church tower (it was later moved to the Church Hall annexe, the Air Raid Precautions room). There were sentries on the quay, and more at Porth Cressa, and a Union flag flying from King Edward's tower on Buzza Hill. Black-out was a problem; the only materials available were black paper, sateen, and oilcloth. Within four days there was an SOS from beyond Bishop and then silence; it was presumed to come from the *Olive Grove*, sunk by a U-boat. Three days after that a Sunderland flying boat landed and taxied into St Mary's Pool with engine trouble. The war was on; by mid-November 150 men had already gone to join the Forces.

When the Germans overran France in 1940 they were only 140 miles away from Scilly. Two boatloads of French refugees arrived in June, and in July came the first air-raid alerts. On 20 July the *Scillonian*, escorted by a destroyer, brought in the first group of troops, a mixed bag of men from many regiments, some back from Norway, some from Dunkirk. The very next day the men were swimming from Porth Cressa beach; it was a glorious summer. Holgate's became the dining hall, the Church Hall a canteen. Some parties were detached to Agnes and Tresco. Pleasure boats, both *Sapphires, Gloria, Nemo* and *Zedora*, were all taken over by the troops, who were busy lining the back of the beaches with barbed wire, erecting poles on the golf-course to prevent planes from landing, and holding anti-invasion exercises. With ship's lifeboats coming in with survivors from sunken merchantmen, and German planes constantly overhead, war was very sharply in the islands.

By mid-August the Battle of Britain was in full rage. The islands were completely exposed. By day planes could sweep in from the sea to shoot up people in the streets and fields, even on the quay. A small girl was killed by machine-gun fire at Telegraph. Incendiary and high-explosive bombs could drop by day or night, and St Mary's, Tresco, and Bryher had all had a taste by 22 August. St Helen's was set alight and burned for days. During the last week of the month there were daily attacks on the island, with little rest by night. The soldiers shot back as best they could with rifles and bren guns. There were no anti-aircraft guns, and no air cover. On 28 August about 150 islanders sailed for the mainland in the steamer. By 31 August about 400 had gone, and no wonder; the soldiers said it was like living in the front line. Even the crossing was perilous, for the *Scillonian* had to edge her way into Mount's Bay past the funnel of a sweeper sunk by mines.

On 31 August two destroyers anchored in the roads to give some fire-power. On 3 September anti-aircraft guns and gunners were brought in. Four days later, at midnight, all the troops and the island Home Guard were called out on a warning of an invasion. There was a stand-to again the next night, and many rumours circulating of enemy barges and troops at sea, being sunk by our naval ships. It was the rumour which swept the south coast, and the nearest Hitler came to invasion.

All that winter and spring the raids went on. The garrison gradually built up, with South Wales Borderers, King's Own Royal Rifles, Royal Fusiliers, and a Scottish pioneer force. In May 1941 the West Yorks replaced the Fusiliers, three motor torpedo boats took up station in St Mary's Pool, and on 19 May No 87 Squadron of Hurricanes arrived. Within five minutes of their landing they were scrambled and Pilot Officer Badger found a Dornier flying boat only 50ft over the sea, which he promptly shot down. By the end of the month they had scored one more 'kill' and a 'probable'. By July there were over 1,000 troops in the island, mainly out in billets. There were echoes of the old Invalid days when the Chaplain of the Isles said after one church parade he would be burying half the soldiers if they did not soon go, they were so old. The oldest was reputed to be seventy-two.

With stronger defences the enemy attacks became more desultory, though the worst raid came early on the morning of 28 August, when the parish church on St Mary's was damaged and two girls killed in a house at the top of the Strand. The airport was enlarged by taking in a flower field, but narcissi continued to come up (as they still do). Even a steam roller was brought in to compress runways, and other vast lorries, of a size unknown on St Mary's, arrived with radar and other equipment. The war settled down, with a little more drunken-ness (one man came out of the NAAFI, walked over the pier-head, and was drowned), more crimes, more trouble than the islanders usually knew. The Duke of Cornwall's Light Infantry replaced the West Yorks. Mystery boats supposed to be making secret contact with French fishermen in the Bay of Biscay slipped in and out. Some Seaforth Highlanders arrived, and the Devons replaced the DCLI. In August 1943 landing craft re-turning from North Africa came in, 'the strangest craft ever seen in Scilly'. Some beached on Porth Mellon, and the men gave lemons, oranges and bananas to the children who played around them, welcome foreign fruit in wartime rationing. Strange planes were landing on the airport too, of unprecedented size; a Wellington, even a Liberator which crash-landed and killed the pilot.

From the time troops arrived in 1940 everyone landing on St Mary's, or leaving, had to face a scrutiny and show papers on the quay. Spy stories bobbed up and down over the years. Early in 1944 the islands, like the whole coast from the Land's End to the Wash, was closed. On 6 June our forces invaded France. The story circulating in the islands was that the airport had telephoned the Home Guard headquarters with a report that paratroops had landed at Normandy. To the islanders the only Normandy was the farm of that name, on the east coast of St Mary's, so all the Home Guard was promptly turned out.

In August the main body of troops went away. In October the airport closed down; on 3 December the island Home Guard held its last parade. Scilly was getting back to normal, though the U-boats were busier now off its shores than at any time. There were several sinkings off the Land's End, one even seen by passengers on a plane from the islands to St Just. But on 8 May 1945 came 'Victory in Europe' Day, and on 10 May the first U-boat to surrender was picked up 30 miles south of the islands. Their war was over.

With its fighter planes the islands had played an aggressive part in the war. Apart from providing local air protection the Hurricanes had limited the sea patrols of German planes, covered air-sea rescue operations, and escorted back planes damaged in French raids. Though one island plane failed to return and seven were lost, or damaged in accidents, their score of enemy planes was six destroyed and four 'probables'. About a quarter of the population of the islands was away in the forces. Even the chaplain, the Rev Edward Seager, went off as an engineer officer in the Merchant Navy. The Lyonesse Remembrance League, largely run by Miss E. P. Rogers, the school teacher and church organist at St Mary's, kept in touch with them all, sending presents, and a copy of the *Scillonian* magazine every quarter. The roll of honour has the names of twenty who died on active service, as against forty-five in World War I. The islands raised over half a million pounds in national savings.

But of all the innovations the war years saw, the arrival of the first jeep is the craziest story. On 24 February 1944 a Dakota crash-landed on the airport, overshooting the runway and smashing up. Out climbed some American airmen and two women. From the wreckage they extracted a jeep, a barrel of cider, and a ham, and careered off all round the island on a joy-ride.

Page 51 Ancient Scilly: (*above*) the settlement on Nornour which may have been occupied from 1200 BC to about AD 371; (*below*) the sanctuary of the oratory on St Helen's, heart of the Celtic monastery

Page 52 Castles: (*above*) the earliest-known view of Star Castle and the beginnings of Hugh Town. The engraving is from *Travels of Cosmo the Third Grand Duke of Tuscany, through England* (1821) but is based on an illustration by an artist who was with Count Cosmo in the islands in 1669; (*below*) Cromwell's Castle, Tresco, with Bryher beyond. The helicopter was delivering old cannons in 1971

4   LANDLORDS AND LOCAL GOVERNMENT

THE COUNCIL OF TWELVE

SO LONG as the Isles of Scilly were an estate leased from the Duchy by one man, local government presented no problem. The lessee, the lord proprietor, was all in all. From Blanchminster to Godolphin times he was required to pay in part for the estate by defending the islands; Godolphins were also governors and as such military commanders. In their absence they appointed lieutenant-governors who exercised civil and military control on behalf of their patrons.

But when William of Orange came to the throne of England he was not going to have a Tory, Stuart-supporting figure in so vital a post and in 1692 the lieutenant-governor of Scilly was appointed by the War Office. He might not reside, but from him the senior military officer drew authority as garrison commander. Equally the lord proprietor was rarely if ever resident though he had his resident steward to guard his interests, and a 'Council of Twelve' who acted on his behalf. This body appears in the early eighteenth century, with the rise of population and prosperity that followed the growth of English merchant shipping at this time. It is clear that by 1738 the military commander was accustomed to sit as president; that this had led to dispute is shown by a letter from Godolphin to the commandant pointing out that his civil rights came from his proprietorship and he doubted if he could delegate them to a deputy appointed by the War Office.

All through the eighteenth century the Council of Twelve, a self-perpetuating body, suffered as the senior soldier and the

D

lord proprietor's agent fought for the chairmanship. The Council had minor legal powers but there were no magistrates in the islands. There was a Collector of Customs with other powers, and the chaplain had his authority. Shipping was increasing, the merchants becoming stronger, pilotage uncontrolled, smuggling rife and looting not uncommon.

In 1783 Godolphin dissolved the Council of Twelve, which had gradually lapsed into a state of inertia, and appointed a new one, with his steward as president and among the members the senior military officer, the chaplain and his curate on Tresco, the Controller and the Collector of Customs. On Godolphin's death in 1785 the lease of Scilly passed to his son-in-law, the fifth Duke of Leeds, who had married Mary Godolphin. The duke re-appointed a similar council, but now with the commandant as president.

This Council faced a new problem. The old Poor Law was administered by the parish vestry, which could levy a rate for the relief of paupers. In 1790 the St Mary's people protested that while they paid a poor rate the off-islanders did not, though their paupers received relief. So the Council resolved that in future, instead of the islands being one parish, each inhabited island should be a self-contained parish. It was a cheap way of shrugging off a problem which was to lay up trouble for the future.

The Council tottered into the nineteenth century with more quarrels between steward and commandant, and an internal battle in 1806 which led to the commandant being recalled and the Council dismissed by the sixth duke. The new Council not only felt itself to be inadequately supported by the duke, but got itself caught up in another interminable wrangle over a Government supply of duty-free salt. By 1817 the duke's steward had been accused of neglecting his duties, and members of the Council of feathering their own nests. The Council, discredited with the Church, the islanders, and the proprietor, lapsed into virtual silence.

The duke's lease was due to end in 1831. Talks between him and the Duchy began in 1825 but by 1829 it seemed certain that the duke would not renew the lease. Not only had his revenues fallen off severely in the depression that followed the end of the Napoleonic Wars, but the poverty of the off-islands had become a national scandal. So the Duchy sent down its surveyor, Edward Driver, to make a valuation of the islands. He found that all the local leases were on verbal agreements, that there was much sub-letting, that much reassessment of rents was needed, that the practice prevailed of all the children dividing a man's lease on his death, so that holdings grew smaller and smaller, scattered all over the place, that all the harbour dues were going into the commandant's pocket and that the military held their land without charge. He came up with a series of proposals for reform, including the institution of a more efficient government than the Council of Twelve.

In October 1831 the Duke of Leeds finally refused the Duchy terms for a new lease and in November the islands returned to the direct control of the Duchy. Not only was the Godolphin family link, which went back to 1571, severed, but the long-moribund Council of Twelve ceased to exist. The Duchy operated direct control and sent down George Driver, brother of their surveyor, to put into effect the reforms his brother had proposed. He induced nineteen farmers to take new leases with a 30 per cent rent increase before general resistance developed. Most farm rents, like most house rents, were in the end left to the new proprietor. On St Mary's a new form of local government was introduced, when a public meeting of the inhabitants in May 1832 led to a general meeting of the inhabitants in vestry, and a select vestry of thirty-four people being elected. This was the old English method of administering parish business. Two overseers of the poor were appointed, the two constables responsible for keeping the peace renewed in office, and a local Board of Health appointed. Next year ten waywardens were elected, to exercise the old custom of calling out the inhabitants to work on the roads. For the first few years the resident agent of the Duchy, William T. Johns, presided, but in April 1835 the chaplain was elected.

But this exercise in democracy was rapidly met by the start of the most autocratic rule the islanders had ever known. A young scion of the banking family of Smith (No 1 Lombard Street, the head office of the National Westminster Bank, is still known as 'Smith's Bank'), Augustus had devoted himself since leaving Oxford to reforming the administration and the people of the parish of Berkhampsted, in Hertfordshire, where his father lived. Hearing that the Duke of Leeds was unlikely to resume his lease of Scilly he entered into negotiations with the Duchy, only to drop out and apparently lose interest when the Commissioners of HM Woods and Forests claimed the islands as Crown property. But when the Duchy established its title, it approached Augustus Smith again, who had also been considering an estate in western Ireland. He went down to see the islands for himself.

Augustus arrived unheralded in the weekly sailing packet, the *Lord Wellington*, and put up at one of the cottage inns of Hugh Town. With an 11-year-old boy, Johnny Dysart, as his guide he set about exploring first St Mary's and then the off-islands. He had conversations at least with William Johns, whose father before him had been Lord Leeds's agent, but otherwise he was a mystery figure to the islanders. Smith went back to London and after months of bargaining agreed to lease the islands from November 1834 for 99 years or three lives. He was to pay a fine of £20,000 on possession, spend £5,000 on improvements in the first six years which were to include a new pier and parish church at Hugh Town, and an annual rent of £40. He was also to be responsible for all clergy stipends in the islands.

In August 1834 an Act of Parliament authorised the appointment of justices of the peace for the islands. Smith consulted with Johns and the first magistrates were Smith and Johns; Major-General Smythe, the lieutenant-governor (the last, for the office lapsed on his death in 1838, and only the second in over 100 years to reside in the islands); Captain Veitch, a half-pay naval officer; John Hall, the Collector of Customs; and Thomas Wetherell, retired from the Commissariat Department. They first met in March 1835 with Smith as chairman.

After considering various sites on St Mary's for his island home, including Holy Vale, Augustus settled on Tresco, choosing a site beside the priory ruins. A deputation of leading islanders met him on his second arrival in Scilly with an address of welcome and a petition that he should ease the harsh measures imposed by the Duchy agent during the interregnum. But it soon became clear that the new man was not only going to reorganise the islands in the way he thought fit, but that he would be ruthless in carrying out what he considered to be for the common good. Although one reason for the Tresco site for his home was that it would cause the minimal disturbance to existing tenancies, it was on Jenkins land and three cottages by the priory ruins were demolished, their walls being incorporated in the east wall of the present pump garden. In the first spring that the new house, the Abbey, was being built, vandals did much damage. His unpopularity was quickly established, and has not yet been forgotten.

Yet Augustus Smith did much to haul the islands, protesting and kicking, into modern times. While Tresco Abbey was being built he set up house in Hugh House, the former officers' quarters in the Garrison. In this way he was in close touch with the Select Vestry. He set about building hedges and roads, consolidating the land-holdings by permitting only one member of a family to succeed, reducing the over-high population of the islands. Young people, for instance, could not marry until they had a house of their own. Some children of large families he compelled to find occupation on the mainland.

Smith moved into the Abbey in 1838. The southern end of the hill beside his house was terraced and the work of creating the now world-famous gardens started. Each year he took one of the off-islands in hand, moving into a cottage himself so that he could supervise the work. So exacting was he that on Agnes in 1850 he directed a certain stone to be built into a certain wall. Two days later he found it had been used in building a pigsty;

the offending Mortimer not only had to pull down two courses of masonry to get it out again, but he was fined 2s 6d. It is said that a group of young men on Agnes tied Augustus up in a sail and left him to drown in the incoming tide, only relenting and untying him as they realised the enormity of what they were doing. No wonder perhaps that to help him in his labours he had his butler, Charles Batchelor, and his footman-cum-clerk of works, Charles Holliday, both men over 6ft, whom he had brought down from Hertfordshire.

The Lord Proprietor lived in the Abbey with butler and footman in uniform, an unheard-of innovation in Scilly. Alexander Gibson wrote of him from personal memory:

> Nature had well moulded him, a massive figure wearing a tall grey hat, a prominent stand-up collar and stock, reefer jacket with telescope slung over his shoulder, he carried the air of a king in every movement and gesture, accentuated if possible when riding his favourite horse or being rowed to other islands in his state barge with its uniformed crew.

No wonder that many of the islanders addressed him as 'my lord', and spoke of him as 'the governor'. There is no doubt of his autocratic approach. A story is told that in the 1840s he found that Francis MacFarlane of Porthlow Farm had built a Baptist chapel in Hugh Town against Smith's wishes. Smith told MacFarlane to give up the key; when he declined Smith turned him and his wife and eleven children out of the farm. Banfield, the principal merchant in Hugh Town, gave the family accommodation in one of his warehouses, whereupon Smith declared that he would refuse Banfield use of the quay. He built the pillars for a gate at the pierhead and gave Banfield a deadline. This Banfield defied, and the gates were never erected, but one pillar still stands opposite the corner of the Mermaid as a reminder of an old battle.

Yet for all his early unpopularity, when he was first elected to Parliament in 1857 as Liberal Member of Parliament for Truro, a triumph was organised in Hugh Town, with the town band, the local gentry, and the leading tenants following him in procession to Star Castle where an address of congratulation was presented. There was a public dinner, bonfires, dancing and fireworks; the off-islands too had their dances and even Agnes had its blazing tar-barrels. It is a far cry from the early days.

That celebration was in 1857; in 1852 in his *Scilly and its Legends* the Rev H. J. Whitfield had written:

In seventeen years [of Augustus Smith's rule] the islands passed from poverty to prosperity without a parallel; there was no mendacity, no unions, no paupers; the land was cultivated like a garden and the port was full of ships; churches were crowded with devout and well-dressed congregations. Smuggling and wrecking were unknown; if these statements are true it is the work of one man . . .

Smith held state at Star Castle twice a year, on rent audit day. At the June audit the landlord offered each tenant the refreshment of a currant bun with a cup of coffee or glass of ale. The winter audit was followed by a dinner where the landlord was supported by the magistrates and the clerk to the vestry. The landlord and six or eight tenants would carve, and the youngest tenants acted as waiters. Tenants always sat in the same seats, and a son would take his father's seat on his succession. The senior tenant always toasted the Queen, the Prince of Wales and the landlord, with a final toast 'to the next merry meeting'. The practice was continued by Smith's successors, though the currant bun has vanished together, one hopes, with speeches such as 'May you live all the days of your life, and die happy after that, sir!'

Smith lived and died a bachelor, which in itself produced many legends. He did not lead a monastic life, though one may dismiss the stories that no woman on the same island as he was safe from rape. On the other hand he did have a bedroom next to his study on the ground floor of the Abbey with an outside footpath winding up through the rockery. It is still there, and no one challenges that Augustus Smith's mistresses found their way up this path of a night-time. It is said that one shopkeeper in Hugh Town was shipped off to sea and that the child of his wife sired by old Augustus founded in due course one of the great national companies. Certainly in his will Augustus made provision for two Tresco women and their children.

Augustus Smith's greatest friend – though this relationship seems to have been quite platonic – was Lady Sophia Tower, a daughter of the first Earl Brownlow. Six years younger than Augustus, she was a vivid, intelligent woman, the product of a long line of aristocrats and artists. She married at the age of twenty-five an old school-friend of Augustus, and first came to stay at the Abbey with her husband in 1847. While Tower contented himself with the shooting offered, his wife was entranced with Scilly and the kingdom Smith was creating out of the marine desert, and for the rest of his life they were constantly meeting either in Scilly or London, and exchanged hundreds of letters.

Augustus died on 31 July 1872 in the Duke of Cornwall Hotel, Plymouth, where he had been moved after being taken ill at a masonic meeting at St Austell. At his own request he was buried at sunrise in the churchyard of St Buryan at Land's End, almost in sight of the islands. He feared that with his death the Duchy would recover the islands. No son could succeed him, and he could not be sure that his nephew, to whom he left Scilly, would be willing to live there. He wanted a quiet funeral but even at 6am there was a strong group of mourners from west Cornwall and boatloads of people from Scilly. The monument which he had sketched before his death was placed not in St Buryan churchyard as he had wished, but on Abbey Hill at Tresco, overlooking both the gardens that he had created and the narrow channel between Tresco and Bryher.

THE DORRIEN SMITHS

Augustus Smith's will directed that the lease should be returned to the Duchy provided that it would pay £20,000 down and £3,000 a year for the remaining twenty-three years of the lease. If the Duchy declined, as it did, the islands passed to his nephew, Thomas Algernon. Algy, a twenty-six-year-old lieutenant in the

10th Hussars, was the son of Augustus's only surviving brother, who had married a Hertfordshire neighbour, Mary Ann Drever. Family tradition declares that Augustus had been in love with her, though she would have nothing to do with him and always refused to visit Scilly. She was the heiress of Thomas Dorrien, another banker, neighbour and relation of the Smiths in Hertfordshire, and, on Thomas Dorrien's death, Robert Smith altered his surname to Smith-Dorrien. On succeeding Augustus, Robert's son added a final Smith to become Smith-Dorrien-Smith, later altered to Dorrien Smith when the first Smith was discarded. A brother who kept his father's name was the famous General Smith-Dorrien of the South African War. Algy resigned his commission in 1874 and moved to Tresco; in 1875 he married Edith, daughter of Lady Sophia Tower.

Though hampered by lack of personal funds (eventually the Dorrien fortune restored the balance) and a decline in the economy of the islands, Algy Dorrien Smith served the community as faithfully as his uncle; with his fostering of true local government and the early days of the flower industry he possibly did as much as his uncle to shape the modern community. The Abbey was extended to accommodate his seven children, and the distinctive tower added. His wife died in an influenza epidemic in 1892 and for a time one or the other of his spinster sisters kept house. The children ran wild, growing up true islanders as familiar with the sea as the land, the five girls as well as the two boys. One daughter, Innis, took over as her father's housekeeper when she grew up, and after her father's death lived for many years in her 30-ton Swedish pilot cutter.

Her father, Algy, died in 1918. For 44 years he had been a familiar figure, striding the islands in his blue reefer jacket and yachting cap, sporting a large military moustache. His eldest son, Major Arthur Algernon Dorrien Smith, succeeded him. There were 14 years left of the original lease but the collapse of the flower industry in the war years had impoverished the islands and many of the houses were in need of repair. Much that wanted doing was beyond the Dorrien Smith resources, and in 1920 the major surrendered the lease, seeking a new one. It was not finally signed until 1929 and was again for 99 years. But it was limited to Tresco and the uninhabited islands, though the major had sought to keep Bryher as well, arguing that the two islands made one economic unit.

The major was forty-two when he moved into the Abbey, a soldier who had served in both the South African war and World War I and won the Distinguished Service Order in the first, as did his brother Edward. Between the wars he had made two plant-hunting expeditions, one to the South Pacific and the other to Western Australia, bringing home much to enrich the Tresco gardens. It fell to him in 1918 to lead the revival of the island flower trade, which his father had done so much to launch. World War II was a grievous time for the family. The choir stalls in Tresco church record the death on active service of five Dorrien Smiths, three of the major's four sons and two of his nephews. When the major died in May 1955 he was succeeded on Tresco by his second son, Lieutenant-Commander Thomas Mervyn Dorrien Smith, who had served in the Royal Navy for nearly twenty years.

Commander Tom was already a member of the Council of the Isles, having a flat in the Abbey which gave him residential qualification. Now he moved his home from Lawton Hall, Taunton, with his wife, three daughters and a son. 'Mrs Tom' brought an exotic note into the Smith blood for she was Her Serene Highness Princess Tamara Imeretinsky, daughter of Prince Michael of Russia. She bore Commander Tom a second son two years after the move to Tresco but some ten years later they were divorced and in July 1967 Commander Tom married Mrs Peggy Worthington, a widow with a son and two daughters. In 1972 Tresco elected Mrs Dorrien Smith to the Council of the Isles.

Commander Dorrien Smith set to work very sharply on his succession, to modernise cottages on Tresco, to bring new machinery into the farming operations, to put Tresco firmly into the holiday trade, and to run the island as an estate which had to be self-supporting. His father had his own way of getting things done, as a story from an island Council meeting illustrates. The postal authorities were refusing to paint the telephone kiosk at the foot of Garrison Hill in Hugh Town grey, instead of the routine red, and the major could not understand what the difficulty was. 'We had no trouble in getting the phone kiosk on Tresco painted grey', he said. 'No, Father,' said the commander, 'you went out and painted it yourself.'

Commander Tom equally got things done his way. He was as distinctive in his dress and manner as his forebears, walking the island in his Royal Yacht Squadron cap and blazer with button-hole flower, walking-stick and spotted red handkerchief to proclaim the countryman. He was an autocrat with a strong temper, capable at times of riding rough-shod over people. But he was a character, different, like the island itself. People who battled with his modernising ideas overlooked that he was the man who had to stake the capital, to take the risks. When attacked on a point he could blow up, but he rapidly came down to debate. 'I could not live on Tresco; not even the air's free over there,' said a woman who has now left Scilly altogether. But modern Tresco stands up very well in comparison with the Duchy-controlled islands. Augustus Smith ruled on Tresco for 38 years, Algy Dorrien Smith 46 years, Major Arthur Algernon Dorrien Smith for 37 years, and Commander Tom, who died in December 1973 at the age of sixty, had held Tresco for 18 years. He was succeeded by his son Robert, a twenty-two-year-old student at the Royal Agricultural College, who became engaged in 1975 to Lady Emma, daughter of the Earl and Countess of Plymouth.

THE COUNCIL OF THE ISLES

It was the first Dorrien Smith, Algy, who played a leading role in bringing modern local government to Scilly, and in keeping them self-governing. When the Poor Law Act of 1832 brought about the union of parishes and boards of guardians to care for the poor, the Commissioners came to the conclusion in 1837 that the isles could be left as they were. When the Local Government Bill which became law in 1888 was before Parliament, the islanders feared that they might under the new device of county councils become incorporated in Cornwall. A petition was sent to Parliament seeking self-rule, and Algy Dorrien Smith used all his influence.

Algy also formed a private company of shareholders and set to work to build a town hall in Hugh Town, ostensibly to mark the jubilee of Queen Victoria. It was not finished when representatives of the Local Government Board came to St Mary's in September 1889 and they held their inquiry in the infants' schoolroom. The new town hall was opened later in the month and was all ready for the new authority when, in August 1890, Parliament approved an order setting up Scilly as a county council area. Two years later the new Council of the Isles of Scilly acquired the town hall from the company.

As from 25 March 1891 Scilly was to be divided into five civil parishes (the five inhabited islands); the vestries of the off-islands and the Select Vestry of St Mary's were not to be affected, and the Council of the Isles of Scilly was to be composed of T. A. Dorrien Smith as chairman and returning officer, four aldermen, and twenty councillors apportioned Bryher 1, Agnes 2, St Martins 2, Tresco 3, and St Mary's 12. The Council became a county council for the purposes of the Sea Fisheries Regulation Act, a rural sanitary authority, and a highway board (although each parish was to be responsible for maintaining its own highways); the Education Act of 1870 was to apply, the Council might borrow money to purchase land or buildings, or to pay for permanent works subject to the usual Whitehall approval, and to constitute with the magistrates a Joint Police Committee.

The *Cornishman* newspaper of Penzance thundered against the clause making Dorrien Smith the chairman, saying the islanders should have been left free to elect him if they saw fit. But when Algy died the Council elected the Major in his place, an office he in turn held until his death in 1955. Alderman George Woodcock then became the first islander outside the Dorrien Smith family to hold the chair, to be succeeded in turn by Mr Roland Gibson, Mr Tregarthen Mumford and, in 1972, by Commander Tom Dorrien Smith. The wheel had turned full circle, though the commander had less than two years in the chair before his death. He was followed by Alderman Sam Ellis.

The Select Vestry of St Mary's continued to be the rate-levying body for the island until 1927, when that function reverted to the Council, and the Local Government Act of 1929 finally abolished vestries and an order of 1930 made the Act applicable to the islands. Because the Council of the Isles is neither a county nor a county borough council, and is indeed the only one of its kind in England, special Parliamentary orders are always required to make legislation applicable to the islands, unless an Act specifically refers to Scilly. In this way the islanders escaped paying income tax until Mr Butler specially brought them into his 1953 Budget, and did not need to have Road Fund licences for their cars until a new Act of 1969 brought them into the net. In each case the islanders sent deputations to Westminster and the Member of Parliament for St Ives, who has represented the islands since the county seats were carved up in 1885, pleaded in debate that the extra costs of island life should exempt them. There were cries of bankruptcy over income tax, but the islanders have survived! There were sardonic grins, however, when the first income tax inspector to visit the islands officially had a rough return trip on the *Scillonian*, so rough indeed that the ship could not berth at Penzance and he had to spend an uncomfortable night at anchor in Mount's Bay. About the only tax escaped today by the islanders is that imposed by dog licences.

The welter of legislation since the war has drastically altered the work of the Council of the Isles. By 1945 the market which had been planned to occupy the ground floor of the Town Hall had become a butcher's shop. The council chamber also served as an office for the three girl clerks, who had to go home when the Council met, and the clerk and his deputy shared a small side office. But in 1950 the butcher's shop was taken over and converted into offices, in 1964 more offices still were added, and by 1974 the total indoor staff had swollen to twelve. With demands for housing and improved education in particular the council expenditure went up by leaps and bounds. In 1945 it was £2,606, by 1965 it had risen to £351,954. Similarly, running costs had gone up in those twenty years from £7,211 to £275,528, and the yield of a penny rate had risen from £22 to £298. The net expenditure for 1973–4 was estimated at £285,259, of which £98,131 came from the rates. There is a considerable element of inflation in these figures, and the grant from central government to aid local expenditure is high. Furthermore, a small council, even with its extended staff, cannot have all the specialist officers whose services are required from time to time.

These problems moved the Local Government Commission in 1960 to consider including Scilly in one of the county districts of Cornwall. The Council of the Isles fought to continue as an all-purpose authority, with extra government grants and the help of Cornwall County Council's specialist officers. Cornwall decided to treat expenditure on the islands' behalf as 'in-county' and not 'out-county'. In 1969 the Redcliffe-Maude Report on Local Government proposed leaving Scilly to be self-governing, with help from Cornwall, and the eventual local government revisions of 1972 left Scilly unchanged, a rare one-tier authority. After the nation-wide changes that followed in 1974, Scilly was left the only local authority in England with aldermen.

CHANGES OF TENURE

The other major change for Scilly in this century was the replacement of the Dorrien Smiths by the Duchy of Cornwall as the direct landlord, on all islands except Tresco, in 1922. Augustus Smith had reached agreement with the Duchy that he might sub-let land, subject to Duchy approval; the new order meant that the sub-tenants became direct tenants, and that the land steward whom the Duchy sent to reside in Hugh Town became the man they dealt with. New contracts were negotiated but many farmers, dissatisfied with the new conditions, left for the mainland. But there were others waiting the chance to acquire land and the empty places were immediately filled. Some farms the Duchy kept in hand and, as an islander wrote, 'these rapidly developed into a part of a huge business concern'. The rent audit dinner, which had ceased to be held by the Dorrien Smiths after 1916 because of the problems of the war, was revived by the Duchy in 1935. World War II, and rationing, brought another gap in the series, which was not revived until 1951.

But the Duchy wrought the biggest change in island tenure in 1949 when it sold its freeholds in Hugh Town. Many of the houses had been originally built by islanders and, like all such island properties, they became Duchy property at the expiration of the lease. Apart from this the Duchy ownership meant difficulties for the Council because the Duchy, like the Crown, is exempt from nearly every Act of Parliament and the Council cannot, for example, use its compulsory powers when it needs land for housing or any other purpose.

The sitting tenants were given the first chance of purchase, at the Duchy's valuation. Some tenants did not feel that they could buy their houses and the Council was anxious to avoid exploitation, for it was common knowledge that there were non-islanders with plenty of money available who had already viewed various properties. It was a momentous sale in island life, affecting 170 houses, eighteen shops, three hotels, two bank houses, the Steamship Company offices, the post office, the electricity generating station, the cinema, twenty boathouses and various stores. The Council was given the open spaces, but the beaches were to remain with the Duchy. By Easter 1959 the sale of Hugh Town was virtually complete, with only a few old properties remaining unsold. Some islanders made an instant profit by selling again at considerably enhanced prices and there was a spurt of private building.

In 1967 a joint consultative council was set up by the Duchy and the Council of the Isles. One of the first problems faced was a Duchy proposal for a new form of land tenure on the off-islands. On Agnes, St Martin's and Bryher there were forty farm holdings, all on differing agreements. On some the Duchy had built the dwelling house and the farm buildings, on others they had been erected by the tenants. The Duchy plan, which the Council approved, was that where the tenants had erected the buildings, they should be paid compensation; that all tenants should surrender their leases for new leases of fifty years under which tenants would have to spend an agreed sum on improvements to the buildings, and that there should be two rent reviews in the period.

So either as freeholders in Hugh Town or as leaseholders outside, and with strong local government, the islands move ahead. The Dorrien Smiths on Tresco provide what might be regarded as a private enterprise contrast with the Duchy's performance as a landlord elsewhere.

Page 69
Tresco Abbey (*above*),
built by Augustus Smith
in 1835–8 and the home
of the Smith dynasty ever
since. The tower was
added by Mr T. A. Dorrien
Smith, nephew and heir to
Augustus, in the 1880s;
(*left*) the late Commander
Tom Dorrien Smith in
typical rig and wearing the
chain of office as Chairman
of the Council of the Isles
of Scilly, presented by the
Duchy of Cornwall in 1961

Page 70 Daffodils: (above) picking flowers at Pelistry, St Mary's, with Toll's Island in the background; (below left) Billy Watts of Parting Carn brings home a barrow-load and (below) Donald May of Seaways packs a box for market

5 EARNING A LIVING BY THE LAND

THE first known farmers of Scilly, the Megalithic people, cultivated wheat and barley in their irregular little fields, kept horses, cattle and sheep, and had some pigs and goats. Farming has continued ever since, taking advantage of the mildest winter climate in Britain.

From the earliest written references to Scilly there emerge brief glimpses of the island farming; two pieces of 'digged ground' on Agnes and three in St Mary's in 1193; seven quarters of wheat paid to the king in 1248; corn, oxen, cows, horses, mares, sheep and pigs taken away from Blanchminster's sixty tenants by those Welshmen in 1342 (see p 30). Leland in 1542 said there were 140 islands that bore grass, exceedingly good pasture for cattle, and that St Mary's bore exceedingly good corn 'insomuch that, if a Man do but cast corn wher Hogges have rotid, it wyl cum up'. With Godolphin farms were established or revived, but corn still had to be imported to feed the people. A century later, in 1669, Count Magalotti said the islanders were growing wheat and corn to support themselves, but the increasing population was creating a scarcity. The islanders made their own beer, and had sufficient cattle so that neither cheese nor butter was wanting. The first fruit trees appear to have been planted at Holy Vale in the middle seventeenth century, and were remarkable when they grew because they were the only trees on the islands.

With the installation of a garrison and the increase in shipping, farming switched from the simple peasant economy of feeding and clothing the family to the more sophisticated business of selling surplus crops and using the earnings to buy deficiencies. So Heath in 1750 recorded potatoes grown in great quantity,

E

two crops a year on some farms. There was little wheat, and flour was imported from England for bread, sometimes to be mixed with ground barley, of which there was a surplus. Barley provided bread for the poorer families, malt for the islands' beer, and the balance was fed to the cattle or exported, either in the form of malt or beer. This was profitable because the excise has never been extended to the islands and so the beer was untaxed.

Little hay was made and the cattle were small. Borlase (1756) says the black cattle fed on ore-weed on the beaches during the winter and would not flourish if they were denied it. Sheep and pigs too ate the ore-weed, and Troutbeck (1793) found that this did not affect the flavour of either beef or mutton, but made the pork disagreeable. Fresh butter and cheese had become scarce by Heath's time. Eggs were plentiful in summer, and rabbits and fowls supplemented the meat supply. Beef, pork, butter, soap and candles were imported from Ireland when the French wars did not interrupt commerce and make occasional scarcities in the islands. Garden vegetables were plentiful and good where sheltered from the wind.

The land was manured with ore-weed carried up from the beaches in crooks on the backs of horses. Horses and oxen were yoked for ploughing, and the corn was cut with reaping hooks. Corn sheaves were built into mows and thatched with straw, bound with plaited straw ropes. Threshing was done as required, usually on canvas-covered boards. Most farms had their own hand mills but there was a windmill as early as the fourteenth century. After Star Castle was built there were two windmills on Garrison which worked for about a century, but the military resented civilians in their citadel and the mills were abandoned. Godolphin built one on Peninnis in 1726 but the miller's wages were often more than the tolls received. The last miller, William Maybee, came from the Isle of Wight but his main claim to fame is that one of his sons, Robert, became an island writer of verse and memoirs, a nineteenth-century character. This mill was superseded by a 'Spanish' mill on Buzza Hill in 1821. The Peninnis tower was briefly used as a signal station until the equipment was moved into the Garrison in the 1880s.

The tower was demolished about 1960 but the millstone remains in the foundations. Buzza windmill ended its service about 1890, when a gale blew the sails away, but the tower remains, made in 1912 into a memorial of the visit of King Edward VII.

Borlase in 1756 wrote of fifteen farms on St Mary's. Holy Vale was in bad shape because the house had been burnt down the year before; Trenoweth was a good farm and Newford much improved. Normandy was named. Agnes was 'fruitful of corn and grass' but the Gugh enclosures were unfarmed. Dolphin was the principal farm on Tresco and very fruitful. Tean had fields of corn and pasture. St Martin's had the best pasture and good corn, but the higher fields had been ruined by blown sand. Bryher seems to have been good for nothing but turf for the fire and rabbits; Samson had a few little meadows but not half enough corn to support its two families.

A merchant from Suffolk who was weatherbound in the islands in 1790 was not very impressed with the farming.

> The land in these Islands is plow'd with little Meager Hobbys, and their other live stock are a few sorry Sheep, poor small Cows, and a pretty good Breed of Swine, but all in general are poorly kept, any more than the Human Species.

On Tresco he found most of the people supported by fishing, piloting, and cultivating a little land by their cottages, just enough to feed their families on potatoes and barley; 'the women often thrash, dress, grind, and bake it all at home'.

THE NINETEENTH CENTURY

With the onset of the war with revolutionary France and the garrison swollen to over 200 men, food became scarce and dear. The sale of potatoes to the increased shipping hit the main staple of the poor. The Council of Twelve tried to regularise food sales and prices in 1800, and to stop the export of potatoes, but with little success. Potatoes bought on St Mary's ostensibly to feed the off-islands were there resold to visiting ships.

After the short peace of 1802–3 the number of soldiers was

reduced and there was a surplus of potatoes. With the disbandment of the Fencibles after Trafalgar the men had more time
for their cultivation. From nearly 3,000 bushels sent away in
1807 the figure rose to a peak of 16,694 bushels in 1813, worth
£1,474. As long as the war lasted the market was mainly Lisbon,
Cadiz and Gibraltar, and our armies in the Peninsula. After
1813, when Wellington crossed the Pyrenees, the figure began
to fall, and though new markets were sought in Italy, the West
Indies, Newfoundland and even Ireland, the overseas trade had
fallen by 1820 to just 1,600 bushels worth £100.

Edward Driver's 1829 report to the Duchy found farming
good; it was not strong enough to support the increasing population but capable of improvement by good management and
manuring. Apart from the seaweed, crushed seashells were used
as a lime dressing. Potatoes were sown from January to April
and yielded 130–140 bushels an acre of good quality. Two white
straw crops were never taken successively, wheat or barley on
the best land being followed by clover. An average crop was
reckoned at 32 bushels of wheat or 40 bushels of barley an acre;
rye (mainly an off-island crop) yielded 20–24 bushels to the acre.
Livestock was plentiful: 112 milch cows and 350 sheep on St
Mary's, and fat bullocks sometimes sent to the mainland for sale.

By 1838 when the Smith regime was beginning to bite, farms
reorganised and everyone driven to work hard, the potato export
was revived but this time the emphasis was on the early crop for
the English market. The lifting season was from late April to
early May with every available man at work. Potatoes became
the main agricultural revenue of the islands. In the peak year of
1853 it was estimated that 1,250 tons had been sent away at an
average of £10 a ton; in 1870 the first consignments to reach
Covent Garden made £280 a ton, though this soon fell to between
£16 and £20. No wonder that every sheltered corner of the
islands was put into potatoes, fertilised by seaweed (which also
guarded against the rare frosts) and manure. Casual workers
were imported to help in the short lifting period; they came with
all their belongings wrapped up in red handkerchiefs and the
islanders called them Zulus.

Farms were still small in 1870, ranging from 5 to 15 acres with a few of 50 acres. Corn and roots were reported as growing well, mainly red and white wheat on St Mary's and Tresco, much barley on Agnes and St Martin's, and the main rye crops on St Martin's too, the seed going to the pigs. Scythes had largely replaced reaping hooks, and small threshing machines and winnowers were making their appearance. Various rotations were followed, using corn, grass, potatoes and mangolds, according to the soil and degree of exposure.

The cattle were much improved, Jerseys having been introduced after 1820 and later crossed with South Devons and Shorthorns. Later some Irish cattle were brought in. The milk yield averaged 10–12 quarts a day from which, after providing domestic milk, 8–10lb of butter was made each week. St Mary's and Tresco also reared store cattle, giving an average deadweight at two or three years of 3–5cwt. Apart from supplying the islands and calling ships, there was a surplus for the Penzance butchers. By the late 1870s beef was being sent to Smithfield. The decline in the sheep population had set in.

Agricultural shows were started in Parson's Field in the 1870s at the suggestion of Algy Dorrien Smith. They reflect the life of the farms, with classes for cattle, horses and harness, sheep, pigs, poultry, vegetables, corn, fruit, butter, straw rope making, spinning, potato packing and knitted stockings (the wool spun and knitted by the exhibitor). There were ploughing matches at Longstone. The weekly market day was Saturday when farmers in frock coats and top hats offered lamb for sale in the market house and fruit and vegetables from their carts in the Hugh Town streets.

FLOWERS

About 1870 the flower industry was born in Scilly. The most circumstantial of many accounts is given by Mrs Honiton in a letter of 1921; in this version William Trevellick of Rocky Hill was growing artichokes and asparagus which made good prices in Covent Garden. Trevellick, reading market reports that narcissi from Holland were profitable, realised that he had common narcissi growing wild in his water-soaked soil. He sent some up with his artichokes and asparagus, and had good returns. Wallflowers were growing on Rocky Carn, in front of his house, so he sent some of these and again had good returns. One of his neighbours, Methusalem Watts at Parting Carn, heard the secret and followed suit. Other pioneers were W. M. Gluyas of Old Town, Richard Mumford of Holy Vale and William Barnes of Normandy.

The Abbey version gives the credit for founding the industry to Augustus Smith. Apart from the 'lilies' growing wild in such profusion that they were weeds in the potato fields, a number of species had been introduced into the Abbey gardens. The story goes that in 1865 he sent a consignment to Covent Garden and was paid £1; from this he urged his tenants to market the wild flowers. Trevellick, a shrewd Wesleyan lay-preacher devoted to Gladstone, was the first to heed his advice, sending off the legendary hatbox of flowers in 1867 for which he received either 2s 6d or 7s 6d, and following this up with a tin trunk full of flowers which yielded £1.

The story of the origin of the flowers is equally confused. Alec Gray, farm manager at Seaways in the 1920s and probably as great a bulb expert as has been imported into the islands, says that the soleil d'or (*Narcissus aureus hois*) is a north African flower grown in England since the time of James I. Scilly whites (*Tazetta ochroleucus*) are from the south of France with many rogues mixed in, known in England before the end of the eighteenth century. Paper whites are a selected type of the wild *N. papyraceus* from Italy, known in England by 1576. Grand Monarque, a form of *N. Tazetta orientalis*, came from China by way of the United States. Of the 'cups', Golden Spur and Irving came from Holland, Emperor and Empress were bred by William Backhouse in the 1870s, *N. obvallaris* was naturalised in Pembrokeshire where it was known as the Tenby daffodil, and the 'double daff' (*Telamonius plenus*) was introduced into London gardens from Flanders before 1620; Pheasant Eye (*N. poeticus recurvus*) has been in cultivation for several centuries but grows wild high in the Alps and Pyrenees. Campernelle (*N. odorus*) was brought to Scilly about 1840 by a French sea captain and given to Mrs Gluyas of Old Town. The island version indeed is that most of the early varieties were brought from overseas by ship captains, to be planted in gardens. In the mild climate and suitable soil they ran wild, and blossomed early. The sols and the Scilly whites were the mainstay of the early days, and are still marketed.

But whatever the origins of the industry, Algernon Dorrien Smith did the research work that established it. From 1881 to 1886 he was importing bulbs by the thousand from Holland, in hundreds of varieties. He set aside 30 acres as trial beds so that the most successful strains could be proved, and built ten glass-houses for forcing experiments. The results of his trials, and bulbs from his stocks, were available to his tenants. In 1881 he made a tour of Holland, Belgium and the Channel Islands to study growing methods. By 1893 he estimated that he had spent £10,000 in building up the industry.

The Smith experience of growing shelter hedges for the Abbey gardens was also invaluable; soon the appearance of the islands underwent probably its biggest change in history as tall ever-green hedges, planted behind temporary wattle and lath wind-breaks, cut up every corner into little box-like fields. Escallonia, veronica and laurel were first used, and now euonymus and pittosporum have been added to the hedges, some varieties so frost-tender that on the mainland they are garden treasures.

An unexpected ally in persuading the tenants to adopt the new industry was the chaplain, the Rev J. H. White. A north-west hurricane destroyed the early potato crop in April 1882 and a few weeks later the chaplain used his pulpit at evensong to advocate flower growing. To set an example he promptly planted up the parsonage garden. One other factor which made a new industry vital at this time was the collapse of shipbuilding and the decline in shipping; men wanted work and flower growing, from planting to picking, was done by hand, requiring no more equipment than a spade.

In 1884 the Scilly Isles Bulb and Flower Association was formed by Dorrien Smith, as a purchasing co-operative, and at his prompting in 1885 the first island commercial flower show was held, the first ever in Britain. The export figures show the growth of the business: 5 tons in 1880, 65 in 1885, 249 in 1890, 600 in 1896. The 1,000-ton mark was passed in 1910. Matthews estimates that by 1891 the annual return to the growers was £10,000, and that by 1896 some 160 million bulbs representing a capital investment of £250,000 were under cultivation. Farmers began to build glasshouses to get even earlier flowers, for the return, like that from potatoes, depended on beating other growing areas into the market. A Royal Horticultural Society report in 1890 declares that while early potatoes were still important, 'it has now been superseded in the financial esteem of the farmers by the cultivation of flowers for the Covent Garden Market'. Even the children had a month off from school in the flower-picking season; the schoolboys knew the seasons of the year as flowers, tatties, fishing and apples.

During World War I the islands had to concentrate on growing food, and a war agricultural committee was set up in May 1917 to see that the farms were used to the highest advantage. Not until 1921 were the farmers free from direction but the next year the agricultural committee was re-formed. Its first big task was to fight eelworm pest, which destroys the bulbs and by 1923 was found to have a firm hold in many parts of the islands. Most farmers wanted a resident agricultural expert, and in 1923 Gordon W. Gibson was appointed, a house found for him at Holy Vale and a plot of land there set aside. His duties were to make variety tests, tests of soil and manures, to try out new crops of potential commercial value, to experiment in treating bulbs, and generally to advise the farmers.

Equally important, the ministry put the Bulb Diseases (Isles of Scilly) Order into force on 1 January 1924, which made it an offence to import bulbs unless they were certified free from disease. The Duchy converted the old lifeboat house at Porth Cressa into a bulb-treating station where hundreds of tons of island bulbs were treated with hot water to destroy pests such as eelworm, narcissus fly larvae and bulb mite. The certified imported bulbs were treated as well. Apart from being cleaned by the treatment the bulbs were also invigorated. One grower who planted 10cwt of Horace after treatment lifted a ton of bulbs the next year. Stronger and earlier flower growth was also promoted. A second sterilising plant was set up on Tresco soon after the St Mary's development.

But the post-war years were not happy. Apart from the up-heaval of the Duchy taking over from the Dorrien Smiths, the flower crop was slow re-establishing itself and by 1925 was only back to the 1896 export figure of 600 tons. The potato acreage was dropping under competition from Spain, and the trade virtually died after 1928 when a mid-March frost ruined the early crop. November 1929 was very wet and brought much narcissus rot, and then on 6 December a storm reaching 110mph swept the islands, a British sea-level record at that time only surpassed in 1966 by 116mph in the Hebrides. The salt spray swept across the fields, badly burned the vegetation and killed completely many of the tall hedges of veronica, euonymus and escallonia.

Flower packing was changing; the wicker baskets of the pioneer days had given way to wooden boxes and in 1930 cardboard boxes were being tried. Rubber bands were begin-ning to replace raffia in bunching. Salesmanship was becoming important; neat arrangement in the boxes in lightly-tinted greaseproof paper was necessary, and special spring flower displays were sent to London. Competition was growing: there were 3,000 acres of glasshouses on the mainland, Holland had increased its imports to Britain tenfold in a decade, and France was sending in nearly a quarter million pounds worth of flowers a year.

But the Horticultural Products (Emergency Customs Duties) Act 1931 rescued the island farmers; in 1931 they marketed a record 1,064 tons of flowers and put the figure up to 1,200 tons the next year. The government also called for improved market-ing and organisation of the industry and the island's reply was to revive the Bulb and Flower Association formed in 1884. Protection cut the value of imported foreign flowers from over £1 million in 1931 to half that figure by 1936, and although the

79

mainland acreage increased under this umbrella, the islands began using pre-cooling (in addition to the sterilising heat treatment) of bulbs to bring on crops to a time previously undreamt of, and began to grow potatoes again as a cleansing crop between flower rotations. But in spite of increased flower crops, returns remained stubbornly low.

With the outbreak of war in 1939 came the appeal to grow more food, as in 1914. In spite of the fact that the bulbs in the fields represented the farmers' capital, and that 150 men had left the islands in the first two months of the war, the switch was made. By late 1941 half the bulbs on Agnes, for instance, had been lifted and their fields given over to vegetables. Greenhouses were full of tomatoes. But the bulbs in the fields, even untended, came up, and they were like gold dust in blacked-out England. One flower farmer in 1941 was reputed to have made £6,000 clear profit.

Then the regulations began. First it was forbidden to use petrol to transport flowers; so horses and carts came back, even on the quayside at Penzance. Then in late 1942 all flower transport was banned. Parcel post and even letter post were used; it was expensive but some people were said to be getting £4 a box of 36 bunches. Men in Cornwall were taking violets to London in suitcases and making £50 a week. In February 1943 came further orders against flower transport by post, rail or steamer; after the mild winter the fields still in bulbs were a blaze of glory enhanced by every hedge and even the rubbish dumps as disconsolate farmers pulled off and flung away the blooms (bulbs are weakened if the flowers wither on the stem). Six men, not islanders, were fined for smuggling flowers on to the train at Penzance. By the time the ban was lifted in March it was too late for Scilly. In the remaining seasons a coupon system was introduced for flower transport. There was much suspicion in St Mary's of smuggling by post, and in three months over £600 worth of flowers were hijacked in transit. This kind of loss stopped in April 1944 when four RAF men appeared in the islands' court; they had been caught with boxes already addressed to merchants containing 300 bunches of flowers in tool boxes on a service lorry being taken to Newlyn. People going to the mainland were not even allowed to take a bunch of flowers in their hand; as they boarded the steamer they had to throw them into the sea. Soldiers, as ever with a keen sense of the ridiculous, paraded on the quay when going on leave with one daffodil held in their hand.

But the total flower acreage was reduced by 50 per cent; potatoes, shallots, broccoli and lettuce became the wartime crops. In the storm-ridden winter of 1945–6 (when for the first time some flowers went by air), early December sols made 6d a flower; in January one bunch of narcissi made £15, and more boxes were being stolen on their way to market.

Food rationing survived for some years after the war and 1948 acreages show the effect of war on the islands. Of 1,500 acres under cultivation, flowers had 320 acres, potatoes 160, vegetables 40, grass 650 and livestock 330. Not until late 1949 were the wartime restrictions on flowers finally lifted, and 17 tons on the *Scillonian* on 28 December was the biggest December consignment for years. By 1952 the flower area was up to 430 acres; by 1964 nearly 600 acres.

The war also brought mechanisation into Scillonian farming. There were tractors on St Mary's ploughing up for potatoes in the spring of 1944 and they spread to the off-islands. The first on St Martin's appeared in 1948, on Bryher the next year. There were 147 tractors in the islands by 1952. With them came mechanical hoes, the first potato lifters, small rotary hoes and, as electricity spread, electric milking. Pre-cooling also became more important in forcing early flowers. St Mary's had a refrigeration plant by 1951 (every island by now had its own sterilisation plant). Anemones, violets and stocks were marketed before Christmas in 1949 and King Alfred narcissi from a cold store were being sent away in mid-January. In one January week 750 tons of narcissi went away. In the autumn of 1950 the flower harvest began in late October with paper white narcissi, de Caen anemones, wallflowers, stocks and calendulas going to London. The first sols followed in November. By 1954 the first sols were going in September. The post-war years also brought a demand for more colour and variety and Rodney Ward of Normandy, who had been the leader of the islanders since the difficult 1930 days, was experimenting with bulbs like Armada, which have a red centre. In the late 1950s he had 300 varieties of narcissi and daffodil in production.

The Isles of Scilly Growers Ltd was formed in December 1957 as a non-profit-making company to buy packing paper, string, fertilisers and the like in bulk, and so save money. After many experiments to find a cardboard box which would stand up to sea, rain, ships and railways, 60,000 boxes were bought in the first season. Scilly Growers, a true co-operative with three directors from St Mary's and one from each of the off-islands, had a full-time secretary by 1965 when 146,000 flower-boxes were ordered. Its rebate to members, 5d in the £ in the first year, had grown to 7d in the £ and £4,200 was paid back in rebates in the first nine years. Changing trading circumstances brought difficulties in the 1970s, however, and it was a blow to the smaller men when Scilly Growers went into voluntary liquidation in 1974.

Four bad flower seasons in succession (the 1959 exports were down to 300 tons) led to a conference being held in Scilly in 1960 at which the major points to emerge were that more flowers should be sent to market in tight bud, that there were still too many small farms, and that the co-operation in research and buying should be extended to marketing. So the hold of the *Scillonian* was thermostatically controlled to keep it cool, and the next delivery of boxes all bore the slogan 'Fresh-cut flowers from the Isles of Scilly'. But 1960 brought so good a harvest that farmers could not stop for the spring flower show; 1963 saw such a rush of flowers that there were 12,000 boxes, 70 tons, on one voyage alone of the *Scillonian*. Men were working night and day and at the audit dinner Lord Radnor, the Lord Warden of the Stannaries, could say 'quite a few did very well'.

In 1962 a group of St Mary's farmers started group marketing as Lyonesse Growers and by 1966 were established as a limited company with the island veterinary surgeon, Peter Mackenzie, as chairman. Their aim was to build up a reputation for the quality of produce marketed under the Lyonesse label and publicise it. Western Growers of St Erth undertook their distribution and in 1966 the new helicopter service was used to speed marketing; flowers delivered to St Erth by 11am could be in any British market next morning. By 1966 they were selling 10,000 boxes a season; the next move was a central packing station at Higher Trenoweth, the Duchy home farm. A second marketing co-operative, Morning Helm, was established with Donald May of Seaways as chairman. With Tresco Bulb Gardens, the Dorrien Smith company, handling virtually all the Tresco produce it could be said that marketing had been rationalised.

But costs were increasing all the time, and returns static, virtually the national farming dilemma. It was clear that there were too many small farms; in 1960 about 200 growers were on farms of between 20 and 40 acres, with some less than 2 acres. The average production of flowers to the acre was much less than the mainland figure, about 260 boxes compared with 750–1,000. Machinery was not efficiently owned on such small holdings, and farming methods had to change to make the best use of machines.

The Duchy showed the way its mind was moving when in 1968 it transferred the home farm to Higher Newford and joined the old home farm at Higher Trenoweth to Longstone. This made Barry Mumford, who had trained as a dentist but came back to Scilly in 1963 to run his mother's farm, the holder of 90 acres, the biggest farm in all the islands save that of Dorrien Smith on Tresco. He was planting in ridges, getting rid of older bulbs for white and two-coloured daffodils, and increasing his sols. Potatoes were his second crop, with 25 acres resting each year on which he raised beef.

At the new Duchy home farm a demonstration station was set up, jointly with the Ministry of Agriculture. Flower returns began to improve; the 1965–6 yield of 120,000 boxes made £174,000 and the 1967–8 figures were 175,000 boxes and £328,000. A 'jackpot' season, said one commentator. The development of machinery, notably of the long-sought-after

83

machine which would lift bulbs, was a great help. A 5-acre field could be lifted in two weeks instead of three months, which in turn made an early potato crop possible in that field. The latest potato harvesters can lift an acre a day in ideal conditions.

Potato growing, which had virtually died out in the dark days between the wars, had been revived in World War II and made more economic with tractors replacing imported labour. The annual crop was back to 100–150 tons in the middle 1960s and in May 1969 the islands were working against the clock to get away their biggest crop for 50 years, spurred on by a shortage on the mainland of early potatoes and consequent good prices. In 1970 they had the market to themselves throughout the lifting period, which finished in the second week in June. What had reverted to a sideline was a major crop again.

CATTLE

The Agricultural Education Committee of the 1920s and its successors also did much to improve the island cattle. A bull society was formed on St Mary's in 1926, a premium Guernsey bull imported, and the first suggestion made that a pedigree Guernsey herd might be a profitable link in maintaining the rotation of crops. But pastures were still going back to gorse in 1933 and the islands had to import butter, cream, eggs and milk in the holiday season. Pigs had disappeared and sheep were only to be found on Bryher and St Martin's (in 1969 some Tresco children visiting the mainland saw sheep for the first time in their lives). By 1948 when the Cattle Improvement and Milk Recording Society was formed, the majority of cattle on the islands were at least 'of Guernsey type' and the islands in 1948 were declared the first attested TB-free area in the United Kingdom. A 1952 survey reported 170 pigs, 5,000 poultry and over 500 head of Guernseys, with a higher milk yield than either Devon or Cornwall (7,300lb a year) and a higher butter-fat content; 210 regular workers were employed on 114 holdings. Milk was already getting a problem, but the Atlantic Dairy was set up near the lifeboat slip with a cream-canning business for export.

By 1954 the all-pedigree Duchy home farm herd of Guernseys had been joined by Captain E. G. Hayes's pedigree herd at Tremelethen, and Tresco was grading its 100-strong herd up to pedigree standard. In 1955 an artificial insemination service was started, and the first resident veterinary surgeon, Peter Mackenzie, arrived on St Mary's. Scillonian Dairies was formed in 1958 by the St Mary's milk producers buying out Atlantic Dairy, selling their milk products locally in the summer months and affiliating with a large mainland dairy which took the winter surplus. This co-operation overcame the problem of so many small producers, making possible a refrigeration unit, new separators, and collection vans. By 1963 all their milk was pasteurised. In June 1968 the islands became the first area in the country free of brucellosis when all fifty-nine herds (about 560 beasts) were found to be clean.

FARMING ANALYSED

In 1964 Kenneth Christopher, manager of the Tresco farming business, analysed the islands' farming economy for *Agriculture*. The figures have varied from year to year since but marginally, and his conclusions are still valid. Of the 1,620 acres farmed, 595 were in bulbs, 6 in other flowers, 283 permanent pasture, 176 temporary pasture, 357 rough grazing, 75 fodder crops, 64 early potatoes, 39 main crop potatoes, and 25 vegetables. The flower-picking season ran from sols in November to iris in May, and was normally a week or two ahead of the mainland season. On Tresco the labour problem is met by bringing in students who live communally in a 'bothy' on the old seaplane station, but at the height of the season every grower is hunting for housewives, grandmothers, anyone who can pick or bunch. The peak demand for labour is usually for the three weeks in late February and early March.

The basic problem still is to break the rotation of bulbs, which are heavy consumers of organic matter. Normally a field is lifted after three years, the surplus bulbs are exported, those destined to be used again are sterilised and some cooled before

85

replanting. Mechanisation now enables an early potato crop to follow flowers but though potatoes clean the ground they are also hungry feeders. Grass is still the best alternative; the Scilly climate gives the longest grazing season in the country, and dairying means that the cattle manure the ground and provide summer milk when the demand is highest.

Christopher's 1964 figures showed a gross margin of profitability on cows of £76 an animal. Flowers showed a gross margin of £264 an acre. The early potato gross margin was £145.50 an acre. As the cow population is about one an acre it is clear the flower growing far outstrips both potato cropping and dairy farming in profitability, but all three earn their keep in the essential cycle of farm life. To the flower profit must also be added the sale of dry bulbs, which when shipped to the mainland glasshouses still flower a week earlier than mainland or Dutch bulbs, and so fetch better prices. Christopher's conclusions were that Scillonian farmers should increase their bulb acreage, make the most efficient use of the labour force available in the flower season, grow as many early potatoes as their labour could lift in May without the bulb crop suffering, and devote the remaining acres to intensive grass production, with the maximum number of cows that the grass would support.

Labour remains a major problem for, though the bulbs can now be planted, lifted, sorted and cleaned by machines, the flowers still have to be picked by hand, a back-breaking job done more often than not in oilskins in winter weather, with hands red and raw from 'lily-juice'. Flower bunching machines, have been tried but found uneconomic; after a few seasons Tresco Bulb Growers went back to piece-rate bunching by the island women in their cottages. With flowers packed in tight bud there is less need for shelter and larger fields can therefore be created.

Flowers look like remaining the staple crop of island farming but as the introduction of flowers changed the appearance of the islands, so modern methods look like breaking down the old system of small farms and small fields.

Page 87 Old pictures of the kelp industry: (*above*) gathering on St Martin's and (*below*) a kelp pit on White Island, north of St Martin's

Page 88   Shipbuilding: (*above*) the 265-ton barque *David Auterson* nearly complete on John Edwards's slipway at Porth Cressa in 1870; (*below*) the last big vessel built in the islands, the 179-ton brigantine *Gleaner* in Tommy Edwards's slip on Town Beach, Hugh Town, in 1878

6   *EARNING A LIVING FROM THE SEA*

SEAWEED has fed the domestic animals and manured the crops of Scilly since the dawn of time; for 150 years it provided the raw material for the islands' main export, kelp. This is the heavy, dark-coloured residue of burnt seaweed and was much in demand for the manufacture of glass in the new prosperity of the late seventeenth century. A man called Nance from Falmouth leased Tean from the Godolphins in 1684 and moved in with his family; in turn he taught his neighbours. To this day Tean grows the best bladder wrack and knobbed wrack, the best weed for the trade.

About 20 tons of weed had to be gathered to make a ton of kelp, which would fetch from £3 to £5 a ton. From March onwards whole families were at work, men, women and children, wading after the weed, spreading it on the beach to dry. Two or three families would share a pit for the burning and each pit could make about 10–12 tons of kelp in a season. So the reward for one family might reach £20 in a season. Wading, carrying the wet weed, and the acrid smoke that drifted over the islands from perhaps forty or fifty pits burning at once, made it an unhealthy and unpleasant trade with a poor return. On top of that much of the business for the merchants was handled by St Mary's shopkeepers who gave credit in advance, so that families were tied to one dealer and always in debt to him. Prices fell badly in the post-1815 depression, a series of gales ruined the weed and filled the pits, cheaper weed from Spain ruined a short revival and the last kelp made in Scilly, about 1835, only made £1 10s (£1.50) a ton.

Most had gone to Bristol or Gloucester, and went into window glass or bottles rather than any pieces of elegance.

THE PORT OF CALL

The century after the Restoration saw not just a demand for kelp; it also produced a vast upsurge in English shipping. The tonnage in the American, West Indian and East Indian trades doubled between 1663 and 1773, the Atlantic was a main highway and Scilly as often as not the first English landfall. In the nineteenth century the world merchant fleet expanded even more rapidly. Sailing ships might anchor in the roads to wait for a fair wind; early steamers often struggled in with their bunkers nearly empty. They might call for provisions, or, in later days, for orders. All this generated activity and employment, and a new gentry grew up in St Mary's. The Banfield family emerges by 1774 and the Buxtons in the next century and the two had a finger in every kind of maritime pie. They were consuls, agents for mainland shipping companies and insurance companies, ship-owners, managers and chandlers, merchants, and closely linked with the shipbuilding that went on in St Mary's for a century. The later half of the nineteenth century saw John Banfield living in Strand House with his offices and stores next door; the premises are now the Scillonian Club. He was the Lloyds agent. T. J. Buxton represented the Liverpool and Glasgow underwriters. He lived and had his offices in the house now occupied by Lloyds Bank. The store he built about 1850 is now the Mermaid public house.

Probably by 1750, when Heath wrote 'every man's small boat is his principal dependence', these maritime activities had become the mainstay of the islands. The boom years began to fade as steam engines became more efficient after 1860, ships grew bigger, and the opening of the Suez Canal in 1869 heralded the end of the sailing ship era. By the end of the century the big ships were steaming past Scilly; the islands were backwaters like so many other once-flourishing little ports.

PILOT CUTTERS

The basic activity was pilotage; bringing ships in through the rocky channels to safe anchorage. It was a rough and ready affair at first, with no licensing. The first pilot to reach a ship brought her in. The Council of Twelve tried to tax pilotage dues in 1701 but they were still finding it hard to get money from this hardy breed a century later. They earned their money hardly; anything between four and ten men a year were being drowned in this trade in the last years of the eighteenth century; on some islands there were more widows than women with husbands. Trinity House began to license pilots in 1810, but the original eight were all St Mary's men; the subsequent outcry forced them by 1812 to license thirty-two and include off-island men.

As Britain recovered from the Napoleonic wars so her maritime trade developed, even faster than before. Scilly pilots, many of whom served deep-sea themselves in their youth, were often capable and licensed to take ships up the English Channel to the Downs, or up the St George's Channel to Liverpool Bar. Pilot cutters were specially built to reach out for business, about 30ft long and half-decked in the early days but fully decked and bigger as the century wore on. Pilot gigs, open craft for inshore work first developed in Cornwall, were introduced. In 1846 there were ten pilot cutters in the islands, each crewed by about eight men of whom two or three were licensed pilots. Ownership of the off-island cutters and their attendant gigs was divided among ten or eleven men in their particular island. Cutters of whom knowledge survives can be tabulated thus:

Island	Cutter	Date of building	Ton-nage	Gig associated	Agent	Linked with Shipyard
St Mary's	*Pet*	1843	27			Thos Edwards
	Atlantic	1844	28		Buxton	Wm Mumford
	Presto	1860	31	*Dolly Varden*	Banfield	Edwards
	Atlantic	1868	39	*Sultan*	Buxton	Gluyas
Agnes	*Active*	1837	22	(replaced by *Gem*)		Thos Edwards
	Agnes	1841	26			

Island	Cutter	Date of building	Ton- nage	Gig associated	Linked with Agent	Shipyard
	Gem	1857	25	Shah	Banfield	Thos Edwards
	Agnes	1857	31	Cetewayo	Buxton	Mumford
	Gem	1875	36	Shah	Banfield	Thos Edwards
St Martin's	Mars	1828	22			Mumford
	Gratitude	1842	22			Jn Edwards
	Queen	1855	24	Bonnet	Banfield	Thos Edwards
	Argus	1859	30	Galatea	Buxton	Jn Edwards
Tresco	Garland	1847	29			
	Dan					
Bryher	Rapid	1848	31	Albion		
	A.Z.	1850	31	Czar		
				Zelda		
?	Waterloo	1830	25			Thos Edwards
?	New					
	Prosperous	1836	20		Banfield (?)	

Thus, most islands had roughly two generations of cutters, the replacement vessels being rather bigger. Latterly too the agents and shipyards on St Mary's not only had their own cutters operating from there, but were linked with a cutter on Agnes and St Martin's as well. The Bryher men were independent, though generally they favoured Buxton and William Mumford. Tresco seems to have been the first island to drop out of piloting.

In the summer months the cutters cruised off the islands watching for ships. About 1860 the *Presto*, which carried five pilots, a captain, and three or four apprentice pilots who worked the craft, put all her men in succession aboard homeward-bound ships until only nineteen-year-old John Hicks was left to sail her 60 miles home. He ran into the moorings under the Atlantic Hotel but could not pick them up single-handed; help came when his bowsprit went through the inn windows.

Often these pilots had small farms ashore as well. Even when working in their fields they kept a sharp look-out for vessels needing a pilot; many a row of potatoes was left half hoed when a ship was sighted flying the pilot jack. The Agnes men were best placed to spot such ships because they lived farthest west, in the line of incoming ships; so they obtained most pilotage business and claimed to have the best pilots too. The Hicks family, most distinguished (with the Leggs) of all Agnes pilots, is said to have moved to the islands in 1800 specially for pilotage work.

Towards the end of the 1860s the number of ships calling was falling off, so the Board of Trade decided to license no more pilot cutters. When the Buxton cutter *Atlantic* was wrecked in St Mary's Pool in January 1868 the Board of Trade refused at first to license a replacement cutter. But even without *Atlantic* there were at that time eight cutters and twenty pilots licensed, and falling demand. The number of cutters fell away. *Presto* and *Atlantic* became pilot cutters at Milford, and *Presto* ended her days trawling. *Queen* was wrecked on Par Beach, St Martin's in 1880 and was finally, like the *Argus, A.Z.* and *Rapid,* broken up. The *Gem* was sold to a Southampton firm as a lobster smack. Latterly the licensed pilots were required to relieve each other on the one surviving pilot cutter, the *Agnes,* which was nicknamed the 'Rooster'. She made her last piloting trip in the 1890s, became a coaster for Captain Stephen Jenkins, and ended her days on Tean Par.

The sailing ship era came to an end as the flower business began; the seamen were farmers anyway and just as the timbers of the pilot cutters became farm posts, so the pilots became flower farmers. As Captain Thomas Mumford of Carn Friars, on St Mary's, said in a much-quoted line, 'I can plough and sow, reap and mow, and sail a ship with any man'. By 1931 there were only two pilots on Agnes and one on St Mary's; under Trinity House age limits Richard Legg of Agnes retired in 1957 and John Horace Hicks in 1961, the last of the Agnes licensed pilots. Roy Guy on St Mary's then remained alone but, apart from the Trinity House ships or the rare cruise liners, the work is limited.

PILOT GIGS

The spirit of the great pilotage days is still kept alive by the gigs. The oldest afloat are the *Bonnet* and the *Slippen,* both built about 1830 by Peters of St Mawes. Their first gig was apparently built in 1790 for the north Cornish coast, and these boats were used for pilotage work from Mount's Bay around to Padstow. They were generally of between 28ft and 32ft in length, 4ft 9in to 7ft in beam, under 2ft in depth. As they weighed less than 7cwt the crew of 7, 6 oarsmen and 1 helmsman, could carry them across a beach. They are very fine in section, flexible in use, good sea boats, and fast. The Scilly gigs also carried leg-of-mutton sails, but there was always a danger in running before the wind of sailing them under. While the cutters would cruise off for pilotage work the gigs would take off pilots when ships were leaving the islands, take pilots out when the cutters were laid up in winter, tend ships in harbour, and in addition act as island maids of all work. They became part of island life and legend.

The Peters family built gigs for Scilly right through the last century and their last was the *Queen*, built in 1903 for St Martin's and designed for carrying rather than pilot work, then virtually dead. But a Peters shipwright, Samuel Tiddy, moved to Scilly at some time around 1849, married a local girl and built gigs on the Strand. His last gig, the *Leo*, was racing in the early days of this century. William Mumford Gluyas built the *Klondyke* in 1877 for the Customs service, but she was bought by the Agnes pilots towards the end of the century and named after the 1896 gold rush (in her early days she only had a number). She is now in the museum at Hugh Town, with sails from the Bryher gig *Czar* (built 1874) and the Trinity House pilot flag of Jack Hicks of Agnes, the last pilot to use a gig. But she is heavier than the typical pilot gigs and was 'the doctor's boat', used for fetching medical assistance from St Mary's. In the same way the *Sussex* was used by Bryher as the doctor's boat, racing across to St Mary's in night emergencies. *Sussex* carried island brides too; the last was Bertha Jenkins in 1929, wearing blue silk and a crinoline hat.

The original gigs carried eight oars but the standard has been six oars, with one or two fours and fives and one renowned seven-oar gig, the *Czar* of Bryher. Always called the 'cut-throat gig' by her rivals, she was deliberately built to beat the other famous Bryher gig *Golden Eagle*. Probably the fastest island gig ever under sail, *Golden Eagle* was paid for by salvage money from the wreck of the *Award* in 1861. Sometimes gigs were named after wrecks which had financed their building, like *Zelda* and *Sussex*. The

peculiar name *O & M* simply represented the initials of her
Agnes owners, Obadiah and Mary Hicks.

The introduction of motor engines after World War I really
condemned the gigs to be left rotting in their boathouses, or on
the banks behind the beaches. After World War II three or four
could be found, a survival from another age, in out-of-the-way
corners, pieces of marine archaeology. Then in 1953 Mr Richard
Gillis, a Newquay pharmacist who had rowed in Newquay gigs
as a young man and with Newquay Rowing Club kept the gigs
there in action, was offered the *Bonnet* by the Tresco men.
Probably built about 1830 by Peters, she had been originally a
St Martin's boat and was named after an old woman, reputedly
a witch, who would wave her bonnet to encourage the crew to
further efforts. Tresco men had bought her in 1920; then in
1953, 120 years after her building, she was bought by the Newquay club for £35, shipped back to Padstow and made shipshape
again. On the same expedition Mr Gillis and his friends bought
Golden Eagle from Bryher for another £35 and *Slippen* from Agnes
for £25. Next year Mr Gillis personally bought *Shah* from Agnes
as well. All these gigs were successfully restored, though other
Cornish clubs which also bought Scilly gigs were less successful.

This activity stirred a renewal of interest in Scilly in their gigs.
The Newquay club and Mr Gillis eventually lent the gigs they
owned to the islands, and since 1962 organised racing has been
resumed, with the few surviving gigs which had never left the
islands back in action. Today's crews cover a mile in just over
7 min. Bryher and Tresco jointly crew the *Czar*, Agnes has the
Shah, and St Martin's at first had the *Slippen*; St Mary's can find
two crews who have rowed in *Bonnet*, *Golden Eagle*, *Slippen* and
Sussex. *Czar*, the 'cut-throat gig' won the first race but at various
times gigs have been changed and honours reasonably well
shared. After the death of Mr Gillis in 1973 the Newquay Rowing Club asked for the return of the *Shah* and *Bonnet*, but agreed
to exchange them for a new gig, *Active*, built specially for them by
Tom Chudleigh after the islands' rowing club had raised £1,500
by appeal for this purpose.

Three new gigs had already been built. Tom Chudleigh, a St

Mary's boatbuilder, launched the *Serica* for a St Mary's crew in 1967, and the people of St Martin's in 1969, when the Newquay Rowing Club took back the *Slippen*, raised over £600 and commissioned him to build the *Dolphin* for them. Pearn of Looe built a third gig, the *Nornour*, for a St Mary's crew in 1971. In the Queen of the Isles Cup that year the three new boats took the first three places.

In 1968 *Serica, Czar* and *Golden Eagle* rowed to Penzance, covering 42 miles in 9hr 47min. The St Martin's men made a crossing to Roscoff in July 1972 in *Nornour*, averaging 4 knots and taking 37hr for the crossing. Each of the 8 men aboard rowed for 20hr.

SMUGGLING

Apart from offering their services, the early pilots found a ready market in ships long at sea for farm produce and beer. It was pleasant to be paid in Virginian tobacco, or Jamaican rum, or Indian tea. Selling this enhanced the profit, full-scale free trade developed with the main selling market on the Cornish mainland, and Scilly had a new business.

A Customs station was established at St Mary's in 1682 and a collector appointed two years later, in spite of island protests. But the 1733 collector had only four boatmen to help him, no assistance from the soldiers in Garrison or revenue cutters, no magistrate nearer than Penzance, and the problem of all collectors that he had to pay the cost of all prosecutions. He clearly got no help from anyone in Scilly, and even with 2,000 boardings a year his seizures were small. A commission of inquiry was told of a large quantity of silks and muslins being thrown out of an East Indiamen's portholes into waiting boats while the Customs officer was being entertained by the ship's officers. The Penzance collector in 1760 wrote of the islands 'there being scarce anything carried on but smuggling'. If a cargo was seized and sold it was said that there were only smugglers in the islands to buy it, and the 1766 collector at St Mary's said 'it is quite impracticable to prevent the scandalous and notorious practice of smuggling'.

As the century went on local craft went into business, sailing to France for cargoes. A preventive man was killed and the boarding crew driven off when they tried to take a Tresco sloop near the Crim Rocks; the crew were tried in London for murder and acquitted because the attempted seizure was held to be outside the prescribed two leagues from land. In 1791 the master of a Penzance smuggler, *Friendship*, killed two Customs boatmen in Old Grimsby Harbour when they tried to board.

Smuggling is a difficult business to quantify because the only statistics are those of seized cargoes, and seizures in Scilly are small beer compared with contemporary mainland figures. Nor was there a market for the contraband in such small islands unless the goods were in turn run into Cornwall. This seems to have been the case, for in 1784 the Council of Twelve ruled that every vessel belonging to the islands which sailed for Cornwall laden with spirits should be forfeit. The naval cutter *Tamer* had been stationed in the islands two years earlier to supplement the Revenue Service; in 1786 the Collectors of Customs took over the cost of prosecutions, and as the French wars progressed so smuggling was steadily suppressed.

The war meant fewer calling ships, and so less smuggling opportunity. The virtual end of the naval war with Trafalgar freed ships and men to combat the trade. By 1819 the off-islands were in an appalling state of poverty – the 'Extreme Miseries of the Off-Islands' was the term used in a report sent to Robert Peel. Increased population, the failure of the potato and corn harvest, the national depression ruining the kelp business, all contributed, but the success of the preventive men in ending the barter trade was regarded as the real reason. Government funds and public subscriptions were sent to help but the miseries continued until 1829, when harvests seem to have improved, though they were not to be ended until after the arrival of Augustus Smith in 1834.

Smuggling was not suppressed. The gigs went into the business and although doubts have been thrown on their having crossed to France for cargoes because their carrying capacity was so small, the oral tradition is strong and detailed. There are stories of rough crossings to Roscoff, the French headquarters of the trade, wild parties there, and rowing back for 30hr in a flat calm. One St

Martin's gig is said to have made sixteen crossings to Brittany, returning to Mullion where Mousehole men took over the goods, so that the Scillonians returned clean to the islands. An ordinance of 1828 which limited gig crews to four oarsmen, though it seems to have been ignored, shows they were in the trade in some way. More effective was the fact that in that year the preventive service had twenty-four officers and men stationed on St Mary's, Tresco, St Martin's and Agnes. An officer on Bryher was stoned and then thrown into the sea when he tried to stop some boats landing suspicious cargoes in that year. But the law was winning; in October 1828 the inspecting commander could report that 'these islands were never known with so little smuggling as this year'. Information from Roscoff was a deterrent too; the *Speedwell* and *Mary Ann* of Tresco were seen there and subsequently caught running cargoes in west Cornwall. Both boats were ordered to be cut up in 1830. But in 1831 the inspecting commander still called the islands 'a complete nest of smugglers' where spirits, tea and tobacco could be had in any quantity at two or three days' notice, with vessels and boats at all times ready to cross to France.

Convictions are a poor guide to the size of the trade, but the only guide. Court records show only forty-four convictions in the years 1834–72, not much more than one a year.

One of the first actions of Augustus Smith on his arrival had been to ask the Board of Customs to release the owners of two pilot cutters, who were in Bodmin Gaol for smuggling, and to free the boats. He posted notices throughout the islands promising to eject any tenant discovered smuggling and there were one or two such ejections; after fourteen years he was able to say of smuggling, that 'the disposition of old stagers in this traffic . . . may not be easy to eradicate, but the rising generation, being freed from the temptation by other employments, a complete extinction of such practices may be looked for'.

SHIPBUILDING

Not until the beginning of Custom House records do positive

accounts of ships built in Scilly appear; the first known is the sloop *Happy Return* of 12 tons, built in 1774 by William, John and Barnett Banfield. By the year 1800 there are records of another seventeen craft, nearly all sloops. Two were over 40 tons, and in 1799 the brigantine *Joseph* of 92 tons was launched. The principal builders were the Banfields and apart from carrying kelp to Bristol and Gloucester the ships took salt ling and pollack to mainland and Mediterranean ports, returning with glass, iron and coal from England, and salt and dried fruit from the Mediterranean. Another twelve came off St Mary's slipways in the years up to 1815, the largest being the brig *Union* of 137 tons. But shipping and shipbuilding were not then of great importance as sources of employment, and of none at all outside St Mary's. The development of Hugh Town as a small mercantile centre meant that St Mary's escaped the extreme poverty of the off-islands. Shipbuilding began to boom around 1830 and has been said to have rescued the islands from their depression; this is not entirely true but it was a major contributor, together with the Smith reforms in land holding and agriculture. The most complete record of Scilly shipbuilding has been compiled by Grahame Farr from Custom House registers and reaches from 1774 to 1891 when the last deep-sea ship was built in the islands. His list gives 160 vessels totalling 15,583 tons; the table below shows the development and decline of the industry.

Decade	No of vessels built	No over 100 tons	Total tonnage	Predominant type
1770–9	3	0	65	Sloop
1780–9	6	0	112	Sloop
1790–9	8	0	279	Sloop
1800–9	4	1	270	Sloop
1810–19	11	2	374	
1820–9	13	1	515	Yawl
1830–9	37	5	2,619	Schooner
1840–9	38	23	4,951	Schooner
1850–9	19	12	2,633	Schooner
1860–9	12	7	2,251	Barque
1870–9	7	6	1,322	Brigantine
1880–91	2	0	57	Fishing boat

Farr has not been able to identify the shipbuilder in each case, but enough names emerge for a pattern to form. The Banfields were the major builders up to 1805 when their name disappears. From then until 1829 only William Mumford is named and there is reason to believe that he succeeded to the Banfield business. Mumford goes on till 1873 and thereafter William Mumford Gluyas appears, his successor. The Mumford yard was on the Strand where the former Holgate's Hotel stands; when the yard was established it must have been at the edge of Hugh Town. William Mumford and his nephew Gluyas after him lived across the road at Lyonnesse House, and their sawpits and timber stacks were on the Porth Cressa shore.

When the shipbuilding boom began in 1830 Tommy Edwards started a yard on the beach alongside Mumford's, on the eastern side, with sawpits and timber stacks across the road where the Methodist Church now stands. From this yard came a total of 6,058 tons of shipping, nearly double that of the older yard and many more of the bigger craft. Tommy Edwards built the biggest vessel ever launched in Scilly, the 528-ton barque *John Banfield*. These two yards on Town Beach dominated the business, but two others developed on the Porth Cressa side of Hugh Town. Peter Stideford was building at the back of the present Town Hall from 1829 to about 1847, and from 1840 to 1870 John Edwards (brother of Tommy) was building at the eastern end of the beach.

Output of Hugh Town Shipyards

			Types of vessel			
Yard	Dates in operation	Sloops/ cutters	Fishing boats	Schooners	Square rigged	Total tonnage
Banfield ⎫ Mumford ⎬ Gluyas ⎭	1774–1891	8	2	19	5	3,508
T. Edwards	1830–78	8	2	17	13	6,094
Stideford	1829–47	1	–	5	–	484
J. Edwards	1840–70	4	3	2	3	1,221

Because the identification of builders is incomplete these figures can only be a guide to the relative strength of the yards, but they probably show the balance between them. The best year of all was 1840 when eight vessels, five of them over 100 tons and totalling just under 1,000 tons, came off St Mary's slipways, but from 1833 until 1850, with the exception of 1842 and 1845, there were never fewer than three ships a year launched. In 1837 there was even a 20-ton cutter, the *Antelope*, built on Bryher, but this is the only recorded vessel built on an off-island.

The output is remarkable for a small community but not unusual for this period in the west of England and Wales. If one takes the numbers of registrations at the thirty-five ports of registration between Milford and Bridport then Scilly emerges more or less constantly around twentieth in number of registrations.

The cutters were built mainly as pilot boats. The schooners, which dominated the slipways from 1830 to 1856, were for the fruit trade from the Azores and the Mediterranean and for a long time they could beat the rapidly developing steamships of the time because they could get into little creeks and rivers close to the fruit groves. Harbour development in the Azores finally let the steamers in there, and led to the eclipse of sail. These island schooners, like most of this era, also carried square topsails on the foremast, averaged about 100 tons, and apart from the fruit runs also served in the Newfoundland cod trade and sometimes made triangular voyages, taking fish from the Great Banks to the Mediterranean or Spain, and home with fruit.

With the fruit trade becoming less profitable, square-rigged ships which tramped all over the world for cargoes began to emerge from Scilly. These vessels got under way in 1844 with Tommy Edwards' 338-ton *Monarch* and the 290-ton barque *Lady Sandys* (builder unknown). Tommy Edwards launched another in 1846 and in 1849 both William Mumford and John Edwards were building bigger square-riggers. The last ship built on the Porth Cressa side was John Edwards' well-remembered barque *David Auterson* (265 tons) of 1870. Two brigantines, the 177-ton *Rosevear* (Gluyas) and the 179-ton *Gleaner* (Tommy Edwards), both launched in 1878, were the last deep-water ships to be built in Scilly. From the timber left over Gluyas built two fishing boats, the 18-ton lugger *Island Queen* in 1881 and the 29-ton *Fortuna* in 1891, the last of all.

All the timber had to come by sea. Each yard had about a dozen shipwrights, with their twelve to fourteen apprentices, and labourers. In addition there were the sawyers and their labourers, and the contract workers, people like the six joiners, the three riggers, the two sailmakers and the three blacksmiths of St Mary's who came in when called. The joiners would rig the cabins and sometimes lay decks and build bulwarks as well. In 1850 Francis Banfield started a 600ft long ropewalk at Porthloo where the standing and running rigging for the ships, and tow ropes up to 16in circumference, were made. It was a busy, lively scene; when Dr Moyle arrived in 1849 he said the music of the ringing blows of caulking mallets sounded continuously through Hugh Town. The roadstead was full of big ships, the pilot cutters in full demand, and all was work, bustle and prosperity.

Boatbuilding was practised in Scilly long before this phase of deep-sea ships, and survived it. Frank Watts of St Mary's, for instance, was succeeded as a boatbuilder by Leonard Hicks who in 1920 at Porth Cressa completed the only steamboat ever built in the islands. She was *Sunrise II*, a private launch for Mr A. A. Dorrien Smith. She was converted to diesel in 1947 and stayed in service till 1955, when a replacement was built at Looe. Leonard Hicks, whose last boats were the launches *Sapphire* and *Sapphire II*, was followed in the business by three of his sons. In 1928 Ernest Jenkins built one or two motor boats on Bryher, and since the war Sam Ellis and Tom Chudleigh have had steady boatbuilding businesses at Hugh Town. Chudleigh built three gigs in 1967–70; in 1967 he also launched a 24ft cruising yacht from the western shore of Peninnis. In 1960 four island men built the 23ft fishing boat *Fulmar* on Tresco, at New Grimsby.

But Bryher has seen the most revolutionary building of modern times. Keith Bennett sailed into the islands in a catamaran in 1957, settled on Bryher, and in 1964 began building his own catamarans. In 1968 he sold three to Barbados and that winter shared a stand at the Boat Show; he completed his fiftieth boat in 1971. He works alone from a solitary shed at the back of the beach between Bryher Town and Samson Hill, looking across to Tresco.

The merchant ships built in the last century were owned by islanders and often officered and crewed by them too. Ownership was, in the English fashion, divided into sixty-four shares, and command often depended on how much cash the would-be captain could invest. Such investments could be profitable and the best voyages paid 30 per cent to shareholders. Two shipping companies were formed in the islands. A fairly typical record for one of the small ships survives in the half-year account for the brig *Kate*, 161 tons, built in 1832 by William Mumford. Between June and December 1835 she called at Alexandria, Glasgow, Milford and Cardiff. The round voyage showed a profit of £527 19s 11d for the owners and £176 11s 6d wages for her crew of nine, most with good Scilly names.

The ships registered in Scilly grew rapidly during the century. In 1825 there were fifteen with a total tonnage of 574; in 1838 fifty, totalling 3,062 tons; in 1851 fifty-nine, 6,843 tons; in 1864 thirty-five, 6,060 tons. Of the registered managing owners in 1864, Banfields had the biggest fleet of thirteen vessels including a number of big island-built ships bearing family names, but even David Auterson, a grocer and draper in Hugh Street, owned two vessels. Some ships registered in Scilly were owned and managed away from the islands, though only one vessel managed out of the port was island-built. Not that all the registered fleet was locally built; of the thirty-five vessels of the 1864 fleet only eighteen were built in the islands.

Often the boys who served their apprenticeships in the island yards went to sea at the end of their time, starting as ship's carpenters and working their way up to master. Captain Robert Sherris, who commanded a larger ship than any other Scillonian, though he never sailed in a Scilly ship, was apprenticed to Tom Legg. Sherris sailed in 1865 in the 1,000-ton *Rimington* as sailmaker when he was twenty. He became the second mate in five years, first mate in seven, passed for master in 1874 and took command of the *Weathersfield* when he was twenty-nine. These boys went to China for tea, carrying guns to fight off pirates, to the Black Sea for grain, Iquique for nitrate, the Chincha Islands for guano, Australia for wool and grain, the Mediterranean for currants and Newfoundland for fish.

As captains, and often part-owners, they would be managers and supercargoes as well, finding their cargoes in port after port, beaching their ships to clean and caulk when necessary. There was great excitement when a Scilly ship came home, often after several years wandering the world; the captain would be first ashore in tailcoat, silk hat and rolled umbrella, perhaps with sad stories of a crew member drowned or dead from natural causes, but always with a crowd to meet him. There was complete trust. It is told of one captain that he walked into Francis Banfield's office and threw down a canvas bag saying, 'There, that's what she's earned this trip'.

But, as steamships took over, the Scilly fleet faded, its masters and men drowned or on the beach with their memories. The last survivors were a few small ketches which ran coal to the islands when required and other cargoes that could be found: china clay from Fowey or onions from Roscoff, even a coastguard's furniture! Peat was the main fuel of the islands until well into the last century: the demand for coal was built up considerably by the glasshouse development in the flower trade but that was short-lived. John Banfield owned the *Star* and *Golden Light*. The Steamship Company had the *Coronilla* and later the *Sarnia*. The Mumford family operated first the *Edmund* and then the unlucky *Charles Francis* as coal ketches from the late 1860s until the wreck of *Charles Francis* in 1908. By the turn of the century the Mumfords were newsagents, drapers and coal merchants, an unlikely but typical island combination; they are still the island newsagents. The renowned Captain Stephen Jenkins, a Bryher man, left the Mumfords to form his own coal partnership of Jenkins and Thompson, originally with the ex pilot cutter *Agnes*. 'Captain Ste' and his later *Mount Carmel* have passed into island lore. The last man in the business was Clent Thomas with the *Emu*, the *Emily*,

Page 105 (above) The pilot cutter *Queen*, built in 1855 and based on St Martin's in the great days of pilotage, was blown up on Par Beach there in 1880, when the business was practically over, and finally broken up for fencing; (below) a modern gig race with *Serica*, built in 1967, chasing the *Dove*, which is more than a century old, into St Mary's Pool. In the background is Carn Morval and Bant's Carn

Page 106
Lighthouses: (*left*) Bishop
Rock. The top of the finial
is 167ft above high water
spring tide but can still be
swept by spray in storms.
The tower has stood in this
form since 1887;
(*below*) Round Island
lighthouse guards the
northern approaches to
the islands and was also
built in 1887

the *Maggie Kelso* and the little *R.G.D.*; he ended the trade in 1924. Now island coal comes in, like everything else, by steamer, but coal was landed from a ketch on St Martin's as late as 1927.

FISHING

Fishing has supplemented the larder of Scillonians since earliest times, as the fish bones, the oyster and limpet shells found in pre-historic middens make clear. But the islanders have never de-veloped much trade in fish, though others have exploited the rich grounds round the islands.

In 1750 vast quantities were being caught in spring and sum-mer, salted and dried in the sun for the winter, but only the best, the dried ling, found a market in Penzance.

In the 1818–30 collapse of the off-islands a national appeal raised £9,000 to establish a commercial fishery. A cellar was built on Tresco, two 14-ton boats were built for pilchard and mackerel fishing and another six repaired; much money went on nets and other equipment, but even more money went in unexplained directions. It is suggested that the St Mary's shipyards were the main benefactors; an island member of the committee built Lyonnesse House and it was rudely called 'Pilchard Square' by his neighbours. A pilchard business did make a fair start but soon collapsed, a Southampton vessel which had been calling for lobsters gave up, and there was little to show for all the effort at the end.

Seine fishing went on, however, as it had probably done for centuries. In this method scad (horse mackerel) and pilchards were taken by a net laid in a half circle from a beach and then hauled into the shallow water. It used to be said that the island diet was:

Scad and taties all the week
And conger pie on Sundays

Each net had its name and its owners, the three St Mary's nets being Friendship, Habnab and Industry. These seines, with those of Tresco, Bryher and Agnes, were shot in turn at Cove between Agnes and Gugh, while the St Martin's net was hauled at Ganilly Bar in the Eastern Isles. The catches were salted down and some went for export. Augustus Smith wrote in August 1856 of 'a thorough deluge of fish', and Algy Dorrien Smith (who arrived in 1875) had to allot separate days to the various nets, to stop quarrelling. The last year of plenty was 1913.

Limpets and shrimps were quite largely exported in the second half of the last century, and some were still going away in the 1930s. Since then shrimping has been little more than a summer picnic pastime. Pilchard fishing was revived in this century, and Algy Dorrien Smith in 1910 provided curing tanks on the pier at Hugh Town, under the present store of the steamship company. At the end of each season Dunns of Mevagissey sent girls to St Mary's to pack the fish into barrels for export.

Up to World War II merchants from Southampton, Brittany and even Holland came for the island shellfish and the French came for a few years after the war. But from 1918 to 1939 the average annual value of shellfish landed at Scilly fell from £8,306 to £2,216, though this was still a bigger return than most of the minor fishing ports of Devon and Cornwall.

During the 1930s the majority of fishermen moved into the passenger launches or other employment and the only fishing since 1945 has been a very limited pursuit of lobsters and crabs employing only two or three men. The catch has virtually gone direct to the island hotels or Penzance; it is not easy to buy fish in Scilly. But the return is not negligible. In 1953 50cwt of lobster and crayfish sent to the mainland made £793. In 1963, with crabs added, 171cwt made £3,933 and in 1973 the sale of 186cwt fetched £12,243. Of this over £10,000 came from 116cwt of lobsters.

A tremendous impetus to the fishing of island grounds came with the linking of Penzance to London by railway in 1865. From 1869 to the 1890s the Mount's Bay mackerel luggers were landing their catches at St Mary's, and they were often joined by 'the Yorkies', ketches and yawls from Yarmouth and Lowestoft. This developed as shipbuilding and piloting died, and the sight of two or three hundred fishing boats disguised the disappearance of the merchant ships. Fishing developed with the new flower industry and, coming at the end of the flower season, used the steamer carrying space when the flowers finished. The arrival of steam trawlers just before the turn of the century, which could take their catches direct to market, ended all this.

The business brought a lot of people to Hugh Town but little work, except for the shops and beerhouses. Sometimes it was peaceful, as when the 'Bay men' from west Cornwall would come ashore when weatherbound and sing Moody and Sankey hymns, standing in hollow circles in the Square or on the Parade. There were rougher occasions, such as the famous fishermen's fight in 1877 between the 'Yorkies' and the Cornishmen. Armed coast-guards had to be called out and magistrates prepared to read the Riot Act, but a few broken ribs and noses were the extent of the damage.

Now visiting fishermen are few. Sennen men came over to Agnes between the wars. French crabbers and the rare Spaniard come in for shelter, or supplies, and are sometimes caught poaching; there were four taken in one week in 1933. In 1956 some Spanish boats made the islands their base while they worked grounds west of Bishop. A Russian fishing factory with fourteen attendant trawlers anchored off Deep Point once. Remarkable now, such things were once routine.

QUAYS projecting into the sea have been needed by Scillonians since they first went afloat, to protect their craft and facilitate getting in and out. Old Town Quay is still probably no larger than it was when the town first developed, in spite of repairs over the centuries and some extensions which the sea has destroyed. The surge is heavy in bad weather; men were probably glad to use the more sheltered Old Quay in St Mary's Pool, built under Star Castle in 1601. Sir Francis Godolphin improved it in 1749 and it could take 150-ton ships; it survives but serves little more now than the pleasure launches.

Augustus Smith started the New Quay in 1836 to attract more shipping; when the Penzance contractor 'skipped out' because he was not making enough money, Smith finished it by direct labour. It then reached out to Rat Island; in 1889 his heir Algy extended it to its present length to cope with the flower and fish trade. The Duchy made improvements in 1926, when the café was built, and in 1970; now the emphasis is on holiday passengers.

The kelp business had quays at Pendrathen and near Watermill Quay, both of eighteenth-century construction, and even one on Great Arthur. When the Pest House was built on St Helen's as a quarantine station in 1764 a cut was made through the rocks so that boats could approach. St Martin's men made the 'Old Quay' not long before 1914 but it was exposed to storms and they then built their New or Par Quay on the other side of Cruther's Point. It has since been reconstructed by the Duchy, who also rebuilt the Bryher quay in 1949 and Porth Conger on

Agnes in 1951. The most handsome off-island harbour is made
by Palace Quay at New Grimsby on Tresco, whose name
probably commemorates the fish cellar ('palace' in West Country
terms) of the early 1820s. The utilitarian concrete jetty at Old
Grimsby was built to serve the Island Hotel.

AIDS TO NAVIGATION

The growth of world shipping, not island needs, brought
lighthouses. Trinity House built their first Cornish lighthouse in
1680 on Agnes; it remained in service until 1911 but is now part
of a dwelling house. Originally a coal fire in a specially built
grate (now in the gardens on Tresco) provided the light and an
early keeper, Amos Clark, was sometimes suspected of drinking
too much to keep it burning. But he found enough time to make
the Troy Town maze on the western shore of Agnes. The light
was converted to oil in 1790 and improved again in 1806.

Three years after the Agnes light the daymark on St Martin's
was built by Thomas Ekins, the Godolphin steward, in 1683;
one can still climb the internal stair if courage permits. Originally
painted white like Agnes, it was banded with red after the
1830 wreck of the *Hope*, whose master mistook it for Agnes
lighthouse. Not for another 160 years was another light added,
then in 1841 a light vessel was placed on the Seven Stones reef,
7 miles from St Martin's Head. The row of cottages close to the
Old Blockhouse on Tresco was built for its crew, but in modern
times the men have moved to Penzance whence the light vessel –
the last one was placed on station in 1954 – is now relieved.

Bishop Rock Lighthouse, 'occupying perhaps a more exposed
situation than any other in the world', was first lit in 1858. Built
in the dawn of the steamship expansion, in the 1930s Atlantic
liners in their heyday raced for the blue riband of the Atlantic
and were timed from Bishop Rock to Ambrose Light, off New
York. Work started in 1847 under the direction of Nicholas
Douglass, and as the rock was awash at high water, living
quarters and workshops were set up on Rosevear, the biggest of
the Western Rocks and 2 miles off. Even here men could be cut

off by heavy seas from food supplies; sometimes they were down to limpets but when Douglass could not work he calmly read engineering and mathematics. On one astonishing night the lighthouse builders gave a 'grand ball' there, with the sheds cleared for dancing, brightly lit and coloured with bunting. Guests came from the islands by gig and sailing boat, and danced to the early hours. The stone ruins survive on Rosevear in a small forest of tree mallow.

Work started in 1847, but the first latticework iron tower was swept away in the great storm of February 1850. So Douglass began again, this time with a granite tower, oak tree shaped. By September 1858 the light shone out, but within 17 months a ¼-ton fogbell was swept from a bracket 100ft above the sea. By 1874 vibration in the tower led to iron ties being bolted to the interior. More signs of damage had appeared by 1881, when it was decided to encase the existing tower in granite, and raise it from 110ft to 147ft. Sir James Douglass, who had helped his father build the first Bishop Light and was now engineer-in-chief to Trinity House, finished work on the present Eddystone lighthouse off Plymouth in 1882, and he moved his equipment to Scilly. A temporary light shone out all through the years of rebuilding, and the new light was first shown on 25 October 1887.

The Wolf, midway between Scilly and the Lizard, was first lit in 1870, and built like Bishop on a rock submerged at high water. To cover the northern sides of the islands, Round Island was given its light in November 1887. Douglass built it simultaneously with the Bishop reconstruction and Trinity Cottages on Garrison above Hugh Town were built to house the workmen; now it houses married keepers on their spells ashore. They have a lonely life in spite of refrigerators and television since 1957, and helicopters which since 1948 have brought food when reliefs have been impracticable.

The last of the island lights to be installed, on Peninnis, St Mary's, is reputedly the result of the naval manoeuvres of 1904. Admiral Wilson was in command of a fleet based in the islands and he set up a masthead light on Peninnis. One night in fog this lamp enabled the admiral to lead the whole fleet into the roads.

On his retirement he became an Elder Brother of Trinity House, and persuaded his brethren to condemn Agnes and substitute Peninnis in 1911.

With the increase of shipping using the islands in the nine-teenth century, beacons were placed on Woolpack and Crow Rock in 1848; more were added and the present buoys installed in the 1870s. Of these Spanish Ledge and its doleful bell is best known; with the red glow of Round Island, the single flash of Peninnis and the double flash of Bishop away to the west they are all now part of island life.

COASTGUARDS

Both the Admiralty and the Customs Department had various controls of the coast-watching organisations in the early days. The first Custom House was built in 1696 in Well Lane, Hugh Town, behind the present Post Office; the second in Hugh Street in 1842. When this was converted into additional apartments for the Atlantic Hotel in 1929, its predecessor was a barber's shop and the Custom House had moved to its present attractive home on the Strand.

When the Coastguard proper was formed in 1831 the main island station was established in the Garrison. There were sub-sidiary stations at Telegraph and on Tresco, Agnes (west of Middle Town) and St Martin's, with auxiliary coastguards on Bryher. In 1845 a life-saving apparatus (rocket and breeches buoy) was brought to St Mary's to be operated by the Coast-guard. In 1856 the coastguards were transferred from the Customs Department to the Admiralty, and frock coats gave way to naval uniforms.

St Mary's coastguard station was one of the first six in the country to be equipped with wireless telegraphy, in 1902, and the whole station was moved to Telegraph, where a 180ft radio mast was set up. The service returned to the Board of Trade in 1923 and was much reduced. The Tresco station closed in 1925 but new coastguard houses were built at Agnes and St Martin's in 1927. Agnes lost its full-time coastguard in 1950. All the islands still have auxiliary coastguards, volunteers who also fill the five LSA teams.

LIFEBOATS

The coastguards also had a lot to do with the early lifeboat service. The first boat in St Mary's was sent there in 1837, largely at the instigation of the Inspecting Commander of Coast Guards, Captain Charles Steel, RN. Three years later she was replaced by another boat from Plymouth, pulling ten oars. Both these boats were housed in a shed on Thorofare. Steel himself was coxswain of this craft in its only recorded service, in January 1841, when the steamer *Thames* struck on the Western Rocks and some sixty lives were lost and only four saved. In 1855 the station was closed and the lifeboat sold.

Not until 1874 did the Royal National Lifeboat Institution decide to reform the St Mary's station, the gap being explained that as wrecks mostly happened in light airs with fog, the gigs could give aid most rapidly. There had in fact been two serious wrecks in the previous three years, the *Minnehaha* and the *Delaware*, in which fifty-eight lives were lost. The loss of the *Delaware*, in desperate weather, saw one of the most heroic of all gig rescue attempts. Ten Bryher men dragged the *Albion* to Rushy Bay, fought the gig across to Samson, again hauled her across the narrow neck, relaunched, and battled out to White Island to rescue the only two survivors.

The 1874 lifeboat, the *Henry Dundas*, was kept in a carriage on Porth Cressa, so that she could be towed to either side of the island for launching. She was first put in the water at Porth Mellon and capsized alongside the quay to show her self-righting qualities. The coastguard chief boatman, Mr Jobson, was aboard and as the boat rolled upright he held up his pipe, still smoking. This craft, with sails and twelve oars, was out within a year when the German transatlantic liner *Schiller* struck the Retarrier Ledges in fog and only thirty-seven of the 372 aboard were saved.

Henry Dundas (*II*), a larger experimental sailer, arrived in 1890 and was kept afloat in the pool. But after one service the crew were asking for a smaller boat, and *Henry Dundas (III)* arrived that October, a 38-footer. There were now two lifeboats in the islands, for in August 1890 the 34ft ten-oared *James and Caroline* was based at Periglis on Agnes. Because there were no horses to haul the launching carriage down to the beach a slipway was built in 1903, and with later extensions it became the longest lifeboat slipway in Britain. The Agnes station had its christening in the great gale of 1891 but not until 1907 were both stations to send their lifeboats to one wreck. By this time St Mary's had a Watson-type sailer and Agnes had had a new boat, the 38ft *Charles Deere James*, in 1904. The wreck was the *Thomas W. Lawson*, of Boston, Mass, the only seven-masted schooner ever built. Carrying a cargo of oil in drums she had anchored in bad weather inside Bishop. Both lifeboats went to her, but mishaps sent both back to station. By next morning she had disappeared, together with William Cook Hicks, an Agnes pilot who had been left aboard. The Agnes gig *Slippen* found three men on rocks; one died from his injuries but two were rescued after William Hicks's son Freddie Cook Hicks (who died aged ninety in May 1972) had swum a deep gully with a rope round him. Annet and Agnes were fouled with the smell and scum of oil for months after this wreck, a precursor of the first great oil calamity of modern times, the wreck of the *Torrey Canyon* sixty years later on the Seven Stones. Her oil, however, never touched Scilly but finished on the beaches of Cornwall and Brittany.

The Agnes lifeboat had a busy time in World War I but the station was closed in 1920, the year after Scilly's first motor lifeboat, the *Elsie*, was sent to St Mary's. She was replaced by the *Cunard* in 1932 and the *Guy and Clare Hunter* in 1955. Boats have changed, but the work has not abated. Between 1875 and the end of 1972 the St Mary's lifeboat answered 138 calls and saved 448 lives, and between 1890 and 1920 the Agnes lifeboat answered 23 calls and saved 261 lives. The long slipway on Agnes was partly demolished in 1926 though the old lifeboat house and part of the slip remain. At St Mary's the lifeboat house at Carn Thomas, between Hugh Town and Porth Mellon, is still prominent; it was built with its slipway in 1899–1900 for the fourth *Henry Dundas*, enlarged for the 1919 motor lifeboat and improved several times since. Apart from shipwrecks and taking sick and injured seamen from ships at sea, the lifeboats have served the islanders in many ways, taking seriously ill people to hospital at Penzance in bad weather, fetching doctors, going out to the Bishop in emergencies.

The island's most famous lifeboat family began with James Thomas Lethbridge. He spent forty years in the service, as second coxswain and coxswain, and died in 1934 at the age of seventy-one. James Thomas Lethbridge first took his son Matthew with him to the *Ardencraig* which sank in the North West Channel in January 1910. By 1919 Matt was second coxswain, by 1925 coxswain, and when he was too old to take the lifeboat to sea he became head launcher in 1956. When he retired from that office in 1970 he had served for sixty years; he died later in the year at the age of seventy-six. From 1927 to 1950 Matt had his brother Jim as second coxswain and they received respectively the silver and the bronze medals of the RNLI for their work at the wreck of the Italian *Isabo* in Hell Bay, Bryher, in October 1927. Jim retired in 1950 and Matt's son, the present coxswain, became his father's second coxswain until father retired, when he took over. 'Young Matt' as he is still known, is a fisherman by trade and served in the air-sea rescue launches of the RAF during the war. Matt's cousin Jimmy was his second coxswain from 1960 to 1963 when Roy Guy (the last island pilot) took over; Matt still had his brothers Roy (bowman) and William Henry (second mechanic) in the boat with him. So seven Lethbridges have been in the lifeboat service; they have seven medals and eight vellums between them.

WRECKS AND SALVAGE

The men of Scilly have a long and honourable record of rescuing seamen in distress, sometimes at the cost of their own lives. Wrecks nevertheless have played a considerable part in the economy of the isles. Both king and Abbot of Tavistock argued in medieval times as to who owned the right of wreck, that is the goods cast up from wrecks, but Scillonians had no doubt.

What came on their shores was theirs. 'Wreckers' in the Scilly sense means 'plunderers of wrecks' rather than 'inducers of wrecks' and there is no evidence of ships being lured ashore or any real evidence of the early light ever being deliberately extinguished.

But even after the arrival of resident Crown officers in the islands, the people felt they had a legal claim to the cargo at least of 'dead vessels', that is ships abandoned or wrecked without survivors. The Collector had to have the Riot Act read in 1774 when he impounded 15,000 bushels of salt from an abandoned Dutch ship, and had to call out the military to disperse the mob.

It is of course the lure of salvage, either of ships or cargoes, that has inspired islanders, on top of the true humanitarian feeling of any seaman for another in peril, to risk themselves and their boats in putting out to ships in distress. Even after lifeboats were stationed in the islands it was not uncommon for other craft to get to a wreck before the lifeboat. Bryher gigs towed ashore two lifeboats containing all the passengers from the Atlantic liner *Minnehaha*, aground on Scilly Rock in 1910, before the lifeboat arrived.

The *Minnehaha* was 'the best bit of wrecking Bryher ever had'. The shore of Hell Bay was littered with cases of everything from harmoniums to pencils. There were even grand pianos and crated cars floating in the sea; one landed on St Mary's Quay must have been the first car (it was 1910) in the islands. Apart from the treasure of the shore there was the eventual arrival on Bryher of the man with the salvage money, all in gold sovereigns in a chamois bag: £500 for the passengers; the lion's share of £780 10s for the cattle. For an island of about a hundred people it was indeed a bonanza.

Agnes men did well in 1903 when the barque *Queen Mab* struck Spanish Ledges. Gig crews raced aboard to help man pumps; and the island steamer *Lyonnesse* towed her alongside St Mary's Quay. *Lyonnesse*'s share of the salvage was £1,250, St Mary's lifeboat crew had £7 13s each, men of the *Leo* gig from St Mary's £6 13s each, Agnes lifeboat £75 and the *O & M* gig from Agnes another £75. All this looks small beer against the £3,000 received in 1745 by some island fishermen who found the *Phoenix*, with a cargo of South Carolina rice, adrift among the rocks. St Martin's most rewarding wreck, and most unlikely cargo, must have been the *Hope* from Africa in 1830; casks of palm oil, over 400 elephant tusks, a box of silver dollars and two boxes of gold dust each valued at £400 were salvaged.

The collection of figureheads on Tresco known as Valhalla belie in their elegance and handsome paint, and placid garden setting, the terrible stories of the way most of them reached the islands. There is the well-built and motherly figurehead there, for instance, of the *Primos*. All her crew were drowned when she struck the Seven Stones in 1871 except for one man, who swam to a hen coop, then found this figurehead and transferred to that for several hours before moving yet again to a ship's boat from which he was eventually rescued. The figureheads and other pieces are a dilettante collection started by the Augustus Smith family, now made over to the Council of the Isles.

No doubt there is much more wreck timber supporting island structures, not all of which had the blessing of the Receiver of Wrecks. And many a house has wreck mementoes still. St Mary's Women's Institute held an exhibition in 1957 of wreck bric-à-brac: a gold bracelet set with gems and enamel from the *Schiller*; beads from Beady Pool, Agnes; a leatherbound Bible in Danish from the *Sophie*; a stuffed parrot which had been the pet of the captain of the *Queen Mab*; silk handkerchiefs from the *Delaware*; various trifles from the 1910 *Minnehaha*; a coconut shell sugar bowl from the *Parame*; a belaying pin from the *Thomas W. Lawson*; a large pewter dish cover from the *Brinkburn* and a silver-plated sugar bowl from the steamer *Longships*.

Everyone who has visited Agnes must have sifted the sands of Wingletang Bay for the minute brown beads which survive the wreck of an ancient Venetian ship. The Keeper of the Ashmolean Museum at Oxford identified them as being made in Bohemia or Venice in the sixteenth century; Venetian galleys ceased coming up Channel early in the reign of Henry VIII so these beads remember a wreck of about 1530. Enough have been found for the Isles of Scilly Museum to make up a string.

The *Schiller* was one of the largest Atlantic liners of her day, and barely two years in service when she was lost with 335 lives on the Retarrier Ledges in 1875. The long cortège of bodies being brought ashore through St Mary's, the mass graves in Old Town churchyard, all made a greater impact on the islands than any wreck of modern times. But she was also carrying $300,000 in $20 gold pieces, and many of the passengers had considerable wealth with them. Divers took the ship to pieces looking for all these valuables and most were recovered. But there are dark stories of bundles of American and German money said to have been picked up on the beaches, or taken from recovered bodies, and of two men, one a German Jew, who went through the islands buying up money from the islanders. Some of the villas built in Church Street, Hugh Town, in the years after the wreck are still whispered of as 'Greenback Terrace'.

The *Delaware* is remembered not only for the gallantry of the Bryher gig men but for her silks and cotton manufactured goods. An island bride's dress was made from the silks, the men had silk handkerchiefs and the women fine shawls. There were other windfalls for the women; one unspecified wreck yielded pink and blue vests, so pretty and fine that most women had one or two. Unfortunately they were small sizes, and the well-built island women could hardly breathe in them. The torpedoed *Eastgate* in 1917 had a cargo of Paris fashions, silk stockings, underwear and perfumes. Beaches and islanders were most elegantly perfumed for a long time.

There was another bottle party the next year when the *Rio Mondego*, the 'port wine ship' was on Town Beach, Hugh Town's northern shore. Few people were without their bottles, and one man had a hogshead propped up in his scullery like a water butt. After the 1910 *Minnehaha*, apart from the pencils which are said to be in the islands still, all the smokers had Old Judge tobacco. The wreck of the *Friar Tuck* in 1863 is said to have kept the islands in tea for four-and-a-half years. The *Sussex*, lost in 1885, was carrying tins of fruit, tongue and other delicacies for the

Christmas market, and the island festivities benefited accordingly that year.

The stories of uncustomed goods are always relished, like the goods themselves. But islanders have worked long and hard to clear ships of their goods and fittings before the sea took all, for no more than the just rewards of salvage. Two men were drowned at just such tasks when the *Plympton*, on the Lethegus rocks off Agnes in 1909, slid off and sank as they worked. There were allegations of looting, proved false, when the *Fantee* went on the Seven Stones in 1949, but a ship deserted and left to the sea is a tremendous temptation. Clive Mumford in his *Portrait of Scilly* says that after the *Mando* grounded on Golden Ball Brow in 1955 the St Martin's football team called off a match on St Mary's because the tide was unsuitable, but it did not stop some of them being seen near the wreck that Saturday afternoon. So were many other people; the captain came back to a stripped ship and while much fetched up eventually in the public auction of salvaged goods, much was unaccounted for.

TREASURE IN THE DEEP

Pencils and pipe tobacco, gold sovereigns for salvage, are all part of island life and folklore, but there is still real treasure under Scillonian waters. In 1707 Britain's greatest loss of life from shipwreck came when a Royal Navy fleet homeward bound from Gibraltar was plagued with a succession of gales and finally lumbered into the Scilly rocks. Admiral Sir Cloudisley Shovell and nearly 2,000 officers and men were drowned when the flagship *Association* and three other warships, *Eagle*, *Romney* and *Firebrand*, foundered in a matter of minutes. Apart from the loss of life, much plate and even more specie went down. In 1736 the *Triumph* from the West Indies went ashore under Garrison on the Steval; the rich furniture and much of the £10,000 in cash said to have been aboard was salved though not all was accounted for. In 1743 a Dutch East Indiaman, the *Hollandia*, lost with all hands off Agnes, was said to have had a quarter of a million silver guilders aboard, as well as 'plate of considerable value'.

Then there is the large fortune in cash that an actress, Mrs Cargill, is said to have had with her in the East India packet *Nancy* which went ashore on Rosevear in 1784. Her body was found, and the mail aboard, but little else. When the worn-out battleship *Colossus* sank just south of Samson in 1798 she was carrying a remarkable collection of Etruscan vases and paintings collected by Sir William Hamilton, husband of Nelson's Emma. Much was salved in those shallow waters, but eight crates were lost. There is still a box of silver and another of dollars missing from the 1810 wreck of the *Amelia* on Crebawethan, a mile ENE of Bishop Rock.

The lure of gold induced men to search for these treasures, not without success, even with the dangerous diving devices of the past. But it has taken the development of modern aqualung diving to start a gold rush in earnest. The first archaeological diving expedition in island waters was led by John Dunbar in 1956. Then, in 1964, the Royal Naval Air Command Sub-Aqua Club from Culdrose, on the Lizard, came down to make a survey with the *Association* as their main target. Among them was Richard Larn, who has since written a book on Scilly shipwrecks. There also arrived the Blue Sea Divers' team of Bob Rogers and Mike Ross. The naval team searched again in 1965 but Roland Morris, a retired diver with a restaurant in Penzance, was also in pursuit of the *Association*. All three groups got contracts from the Ministry of Defence in 1966 to carry out underwater salvage on the *Association*. The naval team located the wreck in July 1967 and found cannon, a few silver coins and one gold coin. In spite of secrecy a bronze cannon brought into St Mary's Pool could not be hidden, and what has been called 'the Scilly shambles' began. All three contract teams were in the field, and all sorts of unlicensed people as well. At one time five groups were working on the wreck. The exposed waters off the Gilstone Ledges, the most southerly of the Western Rocks and wide open to the Atlantic, with a seabed gullied and fissured, are dangerous enough without such rivalry, without co-ordination, and without the explosives some teams used. But the work went on more or less amicably, and an astonishing treasure trove came up in the next year or two. Morris's divers found about 1,400 silver coins in one hole they called Aladdin's Cave, and their find in 1969 of a silver plate bearing Cloudisley Shovell's arms was final proof that the wreck was the *Association*.

The coins and artefacts from Roland Morris were turned over to the Receiver of Wrecks and after the official 'year and a day' delay were sold in two auctions at Sothebys, in 1969 and 1970. Contract holders were declared owners of what had been Government property, and allowed one-third of the value of private possessions and specie. The two sales totalled £22,529, of which Mr Morris received a percentage. He bought in some of the coins and other objects, including a pewter chamber pot, for the nautical museum then connected with his restaurant. The Scilly Museum was another modest bidder, and one of the bronze cannons was acquired for the Tresco Valhalla. But Mr Morris believes that unauthorised divers removed perhaps thousands of coins which never reached the Receiver of Wrecks and will never see a saleroom. However, another team of divers recovered over 7,000 silver coins, valued at £30,000, in 1972–3 from the *Association*. Mr Morris renounced his interest in the *Association* in October 1973 'in disgust' but in January 1975 sought a licence to work on the *Colossus* wreck, which he had located.

A no less dramatic but much less publicised hunt was that for *Hollandia*, conducted by a London solicitor, Mr Rex Cowan. In 1967 he began searching records of the ship in London and Holland; he gave up his practice and settled in St Mary's, forming a team of divers, to make the underwater search. Jack Gayton led the divers, the man who had found the *Association* when in the Naval Air Command Team. After three year's toil, an investment of something like £10,000, and much secrecy, the *Hollandia* was found in 1971 between the Gunners and Annet. It was reported that Mr Cowan had bought the wreck outright from the Dutch government and was not required to hand over his finds to the Receiver of Wrecks. Certainly he had sole rights, and gained an injunction against alleged 'poachers' on the site. About 3,000 coins were brought up, several bronze cannon and many other artefacts. Sales at Sotheby's, Penzance and New

Page 123   Wrecks: (*above*) the 13,443-ton Atlantic liner *Minnehaha* aground on Scilly Rock in Spring 1910. Much of her cargo was thrown overboard to lighten the ship and the islanders eagerly collected it; (*below*) two divers, Terry Hiron (*left*) and Jim Heslin handing over their 1973 haul of coins from the wreck of the *Association* to Mr Eric Brown, the St Mary's Customs officer. Just part of the treasure fetched £33,330 when auctioned at Penzance

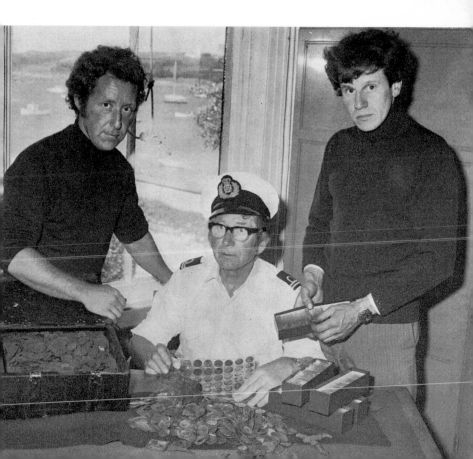

Page 124 Fishing: (*above*) the Mount's Bay fishing fleet anchored in St Mary's Pool at the height of the fishing boom of the nineteenth century. Star Castle is on the skyline; (*below*) Matt Lethbridge, coxswain of the St Mary's lifeboat since 1956, photographed on Town Beach with his crab pots in 1973. The BBC television mast and the martello tower at Telegraph can be seen on the skyline

York produced nearly £100,000. One 'piece of eight' alone fetched £1,300, a world record price. Exploration of the wreck went on.

Mr Cowan's team and others have located a number of other wrecks, including the Dutch East Indiaman *Princess Maria* lost in 1686. She was properly surveyed before her treasures were lifted: 'the Scilly shambles' over the *Association* did lead nationally to much more co-ordination, more control through the Committee for Nautical Archaeology, and emphasis on research rather than mere plundering.

How many ships have been wrecked around Scilly will never be known. John Pickwell compiled a list of 546 wrecks up to 1967 within eight miles of the islands for the Isles of Scilly Museum booklet on shipwrecks, and the museum has his card index of over 1,100 incidents around the islands. Wrecks have been such a part of life in the islands that events are dated by them; even children named after them. Of some little is known, like the two French ships laden with troops sent in 1800 to capture the islands; one sank off Agnes with over 600 men lost. The *Association* fleet is the source of many legends; one largely discounted tells of the Scillonian crewman who warned that the islands were close, and was hanged for his pains (more open to argument is the version that the sailing master of the *Lennox* held that the fleet was off Scilly). Sir Cloudisley Shovell's body was washed up at Porth Hellick on St Mary's, where his sandy grave is still marked (the body was eventually given burial in Westminster Abbey); another grisly legend says that he was still alive when a woman found him on the beach but she killed him for his valuables and cut off a finger to steal a ring. The evidence seems to be that death was from drowning, and no finger was reported missing. Yet the ring is said to be still under the floorboards in a Cornish cottage!

H

8   VISITORS AND TOURISM

MANY visitors have bewailed the agony of the sea crossing to Scilly. In 1242 the brother of King Henry III, Richard Earl of Cornwall (later King of the Romans and uncrowned Holy Roman Emperor), was caught in a storm off the islands and prayed to the Virgin, swearing to raise an abbey in her honour if he survived. The ship crept into the lee of St Mary's, and the ruins of Hailes Abbey in Gloucestershire still bear witness to that traveller's anguish. Storms also brought in Richard's sister Eleanor de Montfort in 1275, and the *Dove* in 1633, westward bound with Roman Catholics who were to found the American state of Maryland. Thirty years after them the Grand Duke of Tuscany sheltered in Scilly; all unintentional visitors.

But the first real tourist suggestion came from Edward Driver, the Duchy Surveyor, in his 1829 report. If there were a steamer, he wrote, 'where one person now visits the islands, many more would resort there, some for curiosity and others as a place of resort for pleasure'. Not until 1858 did steamers come into service, and the following year the Great Western Railway reached Penzance. Now the islands were within 24hr of London. The result was very sharply seen. Augustus Smith in 1861 wrote:

> The gardens are looking very well and are made a mighty fuss about by visitors, it appears . . . they are now invaded by excursionists, which would be a bore, did they not really seem to enjoy themselves and appreciate the place and its peculiarities; some fifty were here this week in a body, from all parts of the kingdom . . .

There were enterprising visitors earlier than this, but the journey was not easy. The railway had reached Plymouth in 1849 and travellers had to go on west by mail coach or by sea.

HOTELS

Captain Frank Tregarthen was then in command of the sailing packet *Ariadne* and in 1849, with his 'bevy of pretty daughters', opened his house at the foot of Garrison Hill as an hotel. It is said that 'rollicking loquacious Captain Frank' would load up with provisions and passengers in Penzance, lump them all in his hotel, and not make another trip till the provisions were used up. Alfred Tennyson stayed there in 1860, already a literary lion with the recent publication of his *Idylls of the King*, and wrote *Enoch Arden* in the hotel garden. Tregarthen's stayed in the family till about 1911 when a company was formed of which Mr W. H. Lane, the Penzance estate agent, was chairman; his son Thurston has been chairman since 1969. In the early days Tregarthen's bar parlour was the club room of the Hugh Town notables, and in spite of major extensions in the 1930s and 1969–73 the shape of the old house can still be traced.

It long advertised itself as the islands' first hotel but there was earlier accommodation. John Edwards's 'Hotel' certainly served for conviviality and meals from 1801 onwards and some of the Waterloo celebrations were held at the Union Hotel kept by James Tregarthen, master of the packet. Both hotels were on The Bank, the little square at the foot of Garrison Hill which was then the focal point of Hugh Town. Bluett's, a large cottage originally, was leased to the Duff family and became the Atlantic Hotel. Then Bickfords from Bryher had it for a spell before the Poynter family from Cambridgeshire took over in 1908. They took in an adjoining cottage and then a shop, and in 1927 leased the 1841 Custom House next door and built a 'public saloon bar' out over the sea on pillars; in 1953 this became the dining room. Mr Poynter was succeeded by his daughter, Mrs Diana Pearce, who sold the hotel in 1973 to Mr Barry Mumford, the flower farmer, and three business men from Truro. The sale price was said to be between £80,000 and £100,000.

What was the biggest hotel in Scilly has had a more chequered history. Hugh House in the Garrison was originally built as officers' quarters. Then it became the St Mary's residence of Augustus Smith and, after he gave it up, became the Hugh House Hotel in 1869. The Holgate family ran it until they left the islands in the late 1890s and Hugh House, after a spell back in military service when the new guns were being installed, finally became four flats let to civilians. But though the Holgates went their name was kept, and in 1899 a new hotel bearing that name appeared on the site of Gluyas's shipyard where in 1891 the last island-built ship was launched. Gluyas was a Mumford and the hotel was built and owned for half a century by Mr E. N. Mumford. Like Tregarthen's it did various military duties in both world wars, being enlarged when first reopened in 1920 and extensively improved and repaired for its 1949 opening by a new owner, Group Captain E. J. Burling. In 1964 because of illness he closed the hotel and simply used it as a private residence. Then in 1970 he turned it over to his friend, Group Captain Leonard Cheshire, VC, to be a rest home for convalescents and staff from Cheshire Homes in need of a holiday. It meant that from 1964 onwards, when tourism was most expanding, St Mary's was deprived of one of its biggest hotels, and thirty bedrooms. Group Captain Burling died in 1974.

These hotels served the islands until 1933 when Edward Bowley, a frequent visitor looking for a holiday cottage, leased Star Castle, which for decades had been the home first of Dorrien Smith and then Duchy agents. Bowley turned it into an hotel; when it opened in May 1933 under Mrs J. E. Stewart the first luncheon guest was the landlord, the Prince of Wales.

In 1967 the Hugh Town butcher, Mr William McFarland Mumford, opened St Mary's Hall as an hotel with his hotelier son Colin as manager; it had been built to Italian design in 1933 by Count Leon de Ferrari, then the bulb wholesaler for the main part of the island trade. The Mumfords took advantage both of the large site opposite the church, and the government grants to encourage tourism, to enlarge the establishment. It was reopened in April 1972 as Hotel Godolphin, with thirty-one bedrooms; the £100,000 conversion had attracted a grant of £25,000 and a loan of £34,000 from the English Tourist Board.

The other 'category A' hotel on St Mary's, the Bell Rock, has also changed its name and been modernised in recent years, but it started business as Fernleigh, one of the few guest houses recorded before 1900. Other guest houses mentioned so early were Mincarlo, Riviera House, and Auriga, though four or five others would take their overflow. These steadily joined the others in the full trade. When Mrs Ivy Roberts died in 1969 it was recorded that Springfields Hotel (closed after her death for conversion into flats) was started about fifty years before when she first took two visitors at her house in Church Street.

BEFORE 1939

Scilly developed slowly as a resort because it had little accommodation, and was a long way from the centres of population; London was 8½hr by train from Penzance as late as 1898 (it is still 6hr) and after that was the 3½hr steamer crossing. One fillip came when Sir Walter Besant set his 'three-decker' novel *Armorel of Lyonesse* principally on Samson. It was extremely popular from its first appearance in 1890 and continued to be published until at least 1949. Jessie Mothersole in her 1910 *Isles of Scilly* talked of 'relays of visitors' helping to bring prosperity. They came for quiet, she wrote, no penny in the slot machines, no brass bands, dancing nor marine parades. There were crowds; in some ten weeks of high summer in 1906 the steamer *Deerhound* carried 6,220 passengers from Penzance to Scilly, an average of 600 a week. Numbers still grow: the 10,000 day-trippers a year on the *Scillonian* in 1960 was 40,000 a year by 1972.

Scilly was included in a Penzance guide book in 1845; and had its own guides published in 1882 and 1897. Alexander Gibson made his photographic shop in Church Street into an 'official information bureau' after World War I and his 182-page *Visitor's Companion in Sunny Lyonnesse* ran into several editions. The 1931 census showed that on an April weekend there were between 50 and 100 'visitors' (non-residents) in the islands.

Probably the number of beds for visitors had grown to 600 by the mid-1930s. If small in numbers they were faithful and frequently returned; in 1932 Jimmy Gould of Plymouth founded the 'Mal de Mers'. A Devon county hockey player, he brought some fellow players with him who in time formed the club, coming back year after year to play island teams at cricket, rugby, soccer, tennis, golf, hockey and snooker. Forty years later they were coming from all over the country, with numbers up in the 1940s and 1950s. Edward Bowley of Star Castle did much to promote island tourism; he wrote what is now the standard guide and in 1945 produced his little book *The Fortunate Islands*.

POST-WAR EXPANSION

The great upsurge came after World War II, with a more mobile public, higher wages and a great spread of holidays with pay. The first flood came in the fine summer of 1947, before the hotels had recovered from the war years. Europe was not the holiday goal it is now, and half the people of Britain were clamouring for their first real holiday in years. Visitors swarmed into the islands without advance bookings; some camped out in 'a druidical tomb'; one islander came down at 3am to find a coloured man asleep in his front room, and others found stranded people asleep in their garden hammocks.

There was a spate of camping for some years after the war, with a hooligan element among the campers. Controls began to be applied in 1950; by 1958 the only permitted site was Sandy Bank outside Hugh Town but as the standards improved so another site on Garrison was added and now there are authorised sites on Agnes, Bryher and St Martin's as well. The Scout and Guide Associations, who alone are permitted to use the open access land, will only permit experienced groups to camp in Scilly.

There was a hippy menace for a spell, an extension of the colonies which steamed down to St Ives. This was contained very sharply when they sought public assistance; they were offered jobs on the island which they were not expected to be able to face; if they tried and gave up, or just did not try, they were given their fare to the mainland and seen off the islands!

But most visitors were well-behaved and welcome, and island accommodation grew to meet the demand. Farms which after 1945 had one or two bedrooms available made more, turning barns and haylofts into pleasant rooms. On a number of farms the holiday makers became more important than flowers or farming. In Hugh Town in particular the number of guest houses multiplied rapidly after the Duchy sold up the freeholds in 1949–50. The Town Hall began to send out lists of accommodation available; 7,676 inquiries were received in 1955. The figures grew steadily: 12,000 in 1960, 15,000 in 1961, 16,000 in 1962. In 1961 it was estimated that 18,000 visitors stayed in the islands during the season.

In 1959 the British Travel and Holidays Association, in conjunction with the Council of the Isles, made a survey of the holiday trade. It became clear that twice as many requests for holiday accommodation in July and August were being received as could be satisfied. It was reckoned that there were at no time more than 1,000 holiday makers in the islands, excluding day-trippers, which still meant one visitor for every two islanders! Even then the report thought that another 300 beds could be made available without damaging the islands. Rather more than half the island revenue was coming from tourism.

Another inquiry conducted in the summer of 1967 showed that of 1,196 individuals only 161 were making their first visit, and the remaining 1,035 had an average of 4·8 previous visits. The Council of the Isles set up a Publicity Committee in 1969 with the initial intention of extending the season earlier into the spring with off-season package tours. By 1970 an arrangement with one travel firm had brought in 150 visitors, and attention was turning to the autumn. The islands, Hotel and Guest House Association had among its members six hotels and twenty-six guest houses.

Examination of the 1974 accommodation list sent out by the council shows 1,333 beds available in the islands. Tresco advertised holiday cottages with another 89 beds, so 1,422 are publicised. Yet there is other accommodation unlisted, through-out the islands. In 1968 it was estimated that there was a total of 2,000 beds on St Mary's alone. But examining the listed 1,422 beds, 845 are in Hugh Town, 372 scattered over St Mary's outside the town, 174 on Tresco, 16 on St Martin's, 6 on Bryher and 9 on Agnes. It is clear which island benefits most from tourism; six-sevenths of the beds are on St Mary's, and more than half the total of all the island holiday beds are concentrated in Hugh Town.

PUBS AND RESTAURANTS

The influx of visitors brought other changes to the islands, mainly to St Mary's. Cottage pubs had been numerous in the nineteenth century but one by one disappeared. For a time between 1918 and 1939 there was only the Atlantic Hotel public bar in Hugh Town but that was closed in 1953, leaving only Jacky's Bar next door to Holgate's. That too has long gone, but in 1954 Mr Rowland Stephenson resigned as Clerk to the Island Council and turned what had been Buxton's Store into the Mermaid, with bars, a dance floor, and immediate popularity. He was his own architect and remained legal consultant to the council, on which he later became an outspoken councillor and alderman. Five years later he sold the Mermaid to the Redruth Brewery, and acquired Star Castle Hotel, which he kept until he retired from the islands in 1972. When Redruth Brewery moved into Hugh Town their Cornish rivals, St Austell Brewery, bought the Nuwear ladies outfitters shop and turned it into the Bishop and Wolf public house, a much more 'townie' establish-ment than the Mermaid.

On the off-islands the New Inn on Tresco was for a long spell the only public house, renowned for its afternoon openings (and even, in times past, for late closing because the nearest policeman was on St Mary's). Agnes had the Little Western in the last century as a pilots' meeting place but it went with the pilots; there was a Turk's Head in Middle Town up to about 1951 but now Agnes has a neat new Turk's Head at Per Conger, near the landing slip. St Martin's had an inn at Lower Town which faded in the 1920s but the Seven Stones opened at Lower Town in 1974. Even Bryher had its Victory Inn in post-war years, but it was closed in 1955 and now it is the only island without its pub. Islanders use boats to reach the New Inn.

Teashops outside Hugh Town come and go as individuals are willing to run them; there were three scattered over St Mary's in the early 1930s and off-islands have had these facilities from time to time. A major boon for day excursionists came when the Sunset Café on St Mary's Quay was opened in 1926. For long it was associated with the Springfield Hotel and is the largest restaurant on the island. In 1973 St Mary's had six licensed restaurants and five cafés.

TRESCO DEVELOPMENTS

Tresco is the one off-island with a developed holiday business. Commander Dorrien Smith succeeded his father there in 1955 and set to work. A row of old cottages at Norrard became the hotel, and it looks like a row of island houses, in spite of the interior luxury. Work started with direct island labour in 1959. The Island Hotel was built in a year, at a cost of £1,800 a bed compared with a mainland cost of £3,000 to £6,000 a bed. Specialist hotel staff is imported, the rest found locally. There are thirty bedrooms, a dining room to seat 100 people, sailing and rowing boats on the beach in front of the hotel, and a heated swimming pool in the grounds. By 1966 Commander Tom, while calling it 'an adventure', said it was paying its way 'moderately well'.

He made a landing charge (raised to 30p a head in 1975) on all visitors to the island. There was some rumpus with the inter-island boatmen but all settled down; the number of day visitors has not been affected, and the yield by 1966 was £2,000 a year, enough to pay the interest on capital invested in the island, as Commander Tom put it. Then two flats were made available in the abbey for holiday makers, and eleven cottages converted by 1973 for holiday visitors cooking and keeping themselves. Each can accommodate between four and twelve people, and are let for sums ranging from £15 a week in mid-winter to £85 a week in high summer. There can be a waiting list of years for the peak holiday times. Commander Dorrien Smith also took the New Inn into direct management in 1969 and modernised its hotel side; a wooden annexe became a pleasant building. A gift-cum-tea shop on the quay at New Grimsby brings more visitor money into the island coffers. At Old Grimsby John Hamilton sells pictures, perfume and jewellery to visitors, all island-made and providing piece work at home for many island women.

HOLIDAY LAUNCHES

The key to tourism in the islands is the service of the inter-island launches. Geoffrey Jellicoe summed it up in his *Landscape Charter for the Isles of Scilly*, commissioned by the Council of the Isles and published in 1965:

> . . . St Mary's, where visitors first arrive, is merely a stepping stone to the real attraction; for St Mary's, romantic though it is, is today little more than a detached fragment of the mainland. But as a stepping stone, a half way post between the two worlds, it is invaluable. It is the four Off Islands, surrounded by the uninhabited islands, that primarily remain in the memory.

Until the early years of this century the islands were explored leisurely by sailing boat. Visitors were then better off and would sometimes hire a boat by the week regardless of how much they used it.

Eustace Thomas, coxswain of the lifeboat and a pilot, had a motor boat, the *Narcissus*, by 1909 though the claim for the first motor boat is made by both the *Cambridge*, owned by Holgate's Hotel, and the Atlantic Hotel's *White Hope*. Later the Atlantic had the *White Heather* as well. The steamship company was advertising summer pleasure trips in its inter-island launches by 1925. As tourism built up so did the launch fleet. Vernon Thompson bought the *Springfield* in 1933 and had the *Nemo* as well soon after, and Leonard Hicks built *Sapphire* and *Sapphire II* just before his retirement in about 1933. Back from wartime service in 1946

were the *Zedora* and *White Hope, Sapphire* and *Heather, Springfield*
and *Nemo*. Vernon Thompson, also back from five years in the
Merchant Navy, made do with a borrowed boat until he and
his brother Cecil could fetch *Springfield* back from the Royal
Navy at Plymouth; she operated in naval grey all that summer.
The renowned Horace Nicholls was coxswain of the steamship
company's *Golden Spray* by 1948. The Thompson brothers (adding *Kingsley* to their fleet), Leonard Hicks junior and his sons,
and the steamship company launches dominated the trade, but
as trade grew (the steamship company added two craft to their
pleasure fleet in 1957) competition crept in and became fierce.

The launches and the crews were brought under control in
1957, when the boat owners and the steamship company pooled
their craft, with a ticket office on the Old Quay replacing touting
in the street and return journeys permitted on any craft. The
system is still working well, with ten launches in the association
in 1970 and only one outsider, appropriately the *Buccaneer*. But
the business of embarking up to 800 people in half an hour 'goes
like clockwork' and it was estimated after ten years that over a
million people had been carried, all in safety.

The pattern is well established; launches leave St Mary's
Quay at 10.15am for the various off-islands, returning at lunch-
time and off again at 2.15pm, leaving the off-islands about
4.30pm for St Mary's. The hurried march of visitors through
Hugh Town at 10 every morning, and their drift back through
the street soon after 5 in the afternoon is part of the island ritual.
Most St Mary's establishments regard a packed lunch for their
guests as normal service.

People have their favourite boats of course and perhaps stay
with one launch for a whole week, for they vary their itinerary
from day to day. To be greeted by the boatmen, to be talked to,
to be allowed the place of honour by the wheel, is as eagerly
sought as a nod from the maître d'hôtel in any great restaurant.
Lady Vyvyan was scathing about the 'launch lizards', as she
called the crews in her 1953 *Isles of Scilly*. 'Slim and plausible',
she called them, 'cigarette between the lips, coiling a rope,
handling a boat hook . . . handing the visitors one by one on to

the slippery seaweed or the wet sand, with sly attempts, on the younger girls, at horseplay and gallantry.' But the visitors love it, the young girls and some of their mothers too. There are dark stories of bearded boatmen welcome not only in Scilly holiday flats but London bedrooms too. But these gallants are now all tested seamen.

Until the Tresco developments all the pleasure launches were St Mary's based; then Bryher came into the picture. Kenneth Jenkins and Vernon Hicks both had a launch in 1960; then in 1963 Leonard Jenkins brought the *Commodore* down from Bristol and the following year David Stedeford bought the *Falcon*. In 1965 Leonard and David combined with their two boats and provided a regular service from Bryher and Tresco to the other off-islands and St Mary's and made the conventional Bishop-Rock-to-see-the-seals trips. In spring 1966 Vernon and Michael Hicks of Tresco brought the *Sea Horse* from the mainland and David Langton added the *Unity*. Commander Dorrien Smith's efforts were helping both islands.

NEW RESIDENTS

Bryher also had its holiday makers. About a dozen cottages had been leased by non-islanders who used them as holiday cottages and let them out when not there themselves. The same thing is happening more or less on all the other islands. After poor flower seasons in 1959 and again in 1966 the Council of the Isles agreed to holiday chalets being erected; by 1974 there were eleven, mainly on St Mary's, for holiday rentals but there are a few more about the islands not listed. These are less resented by islanders than the cottages taken over by non-islanders, but the second homes which take from the basic housing stock are a national problem and a natural result of depopulation; the alternative would often be to see the cottages fall down.

There are distinguished names among these in-comers. The 1943 Debrett's *Peerages*, for instance, shows that one of the 'seats' of the fifth Earl of Onslow was 'St Agnes Island, Scilly'. While staying on Tresco in 1918 he heard that the lighthouse on Agnes was to let, and took the lease in 1920. He and his family spent much time there and his son, who became the sixth earl, attended Agnes school at times. After the death of the fifth earl in 1945 his son took a lease of the Parsonage, one condition being that he should afford hospitality to visiting clergymen. With his death in 1971 the fifty-year link ended, but in the last ten years of his life the earl and countess – Arthur and Jo to most islanders – spent at least six months a year on Agnes.

Miss Yvonne Lucas Tooth and her sister, two daughters of Sir Robert Lucas Tooth, bought the coastguard cottages on Bryher in 1926 and made them into their home. In 1932 Miss Lucas Tooth married Wing Commander Spencer Booth and four years later her niece married Commander Tom's elder brother, Captain Algernon Dorrien Smith, who was killed in 1940. After Mrs Spencer Booth's death in 1967 the contents of the cottage were sold by auction in Penzance for £25,000, one George III silver gilt tray alone making £2,400.

St Martin's also has a remarkable resident in Mr A. H. Dallimore, reputedly a self-made millionaire. He first took the lease of Churchtown farm and in 1962–3 built for himself the New House, said to have cost £20,000. He has leased other small holdings to add to his flower farm and with 30 acres is the biggest farmer on the island, employing five men. Mr Dallimore has built three cottages for his staff and expects to build more; he has a small motor sailer yacht which he occasionally sails to the mainland. He has not set up as an island benefactor and is modest about his part in the island economy, but when he stood for the Council of the Isles in 1973, St Martin's put him top of the poll. Mr Dallimore has enabled the Duchy to follow its present policy of increasing the size of individual farm holdings: he clearly represents an influx of capital into an island not otherwise well blessed.

But inevitably St Mary's has the main crop of distinguished people with holiday homes, and most publicity has been devoted to Harold Wilson. He and his family made their first visit in 1952. Seven years later they built a bungalow, Lowenva, near the hospital, for £2,500. Four years later Mr Wilson became

Leader of the Labour Party, and was Prime Minister 1964–70, and again in 1974. He had become established in the islands well before he reached Downing Street, with his family a regular in most Parliamentary vacations, joining the Scillonian Club, smoking his celebrated pipe in the Mermaid, enjoying the islands much as do other family men. In the years of office he endeavoured to continue as he had always done, and only the eternal detective with the family showed the difference. Naturally he became one of the sights to see, as much as the Bishop Light, and in time had to take over *Nemo* as a private launch to ensure some privacy.

But of course there were press men to meet him on the journey down and up, receptions by the chairman of the Council of the Isles (Tregarthen Mumford is a close friend and golfing companion), little honours like reading the lesson in church (though the family commonly used the Methodist Church), a cypher teleprinter set up in the Custom House with operators specially brought down, walkie-talkie accompaniments in times of pressure on off-island visits. Michael Stewart, the Foreign Secretary, and Ray Gunter, the Minister of Labour, in Mr Wilson's first administration, were regular visitors, and Mr Gunter eventually became the tenant of a new house at Old Town.

The visitors who book their holiday for the following year at the end of their stay, and come again and again, are part of the island pattern; so are those who eventually find holiday cottages which become summer homes and, on retirement, full-time homes. Lord Franks, Provost of Worcester College, Oxford, and in his time Ambassador to Washington and chairman of Lloyds Bank, and Lady Franks first stayed at Parting Carn; by 1960 they had built a house, Somewhere, at Old Town. Charles Cooper, after thirty years as borough engineer of Wimbledon, leased Gugh, built the farmhouse which still stands there, and in 1932 was buried just below the topmost point of the island. Dr A. T. J. Dollar, the geologist of Birbeck College, London, has a house at Porth Cressa. Professor L. A. Harvey, one-time head of the zoology department of Exeter University, had a holiday house on the Garrison to which he and his wife eventually retired altogether. Mr Kenneth Sisam first visited the islands after World War I; when he retired in 1947 from his post of Secretary to the Delegates of the Clarendon Press he built a house at Tolman Point near Old Town. Sisam, who died in 1971, brought his great scholarship to bear on early island history, even as Dr Dollar and Dr Harvey have made contributions in their own fields.

Hunting down the famous among less regular visitors could be tedious, but they include Frank Cousins, the former trade union leader; Fred Peart, sometime Minister of Agriculture; Dame Barbara Hepworth, the sculptor (who broke her leg at St Mary's Airport in 1967); Sir Alec Guinness, the actor; Count de Lesseps, descendant of the builder of the Suez Canal; Osbert Lancaster, the artist; in earlier days the great Dr Grenfell of Labrador. An islander reeling off names of people he had met was told 'You've listed almost the entire royal family, and half the bloody Cabinet'.

ROYAL VISITORS

With the islands so long in royal hands it is not surprising that they have enjoyed many royal visitors; to some extent the visits become those of inspecting landlords. If the visit of Athelstan in 936 is to be believed there is a long tradition. Charles I when Prince of Wales came in with the ill-famed Duke of Buckingham in 1623 to escape bad weather. His son was there as a boy in the closing stages of the Civil War.

When the twenty-eight-year-old Queen Victoria called with the Prince Consort in 1847, Augustus Smith brought his carriage over from Tresco; coming back down the steep Garrison Hill from Star Castle the carriage nearly ran away. Alarmed, the Queen jumped out with Prince Albert at her heels, and the pair walked straight back to the royal yacht's barge. The tenants, lining the quay with white wands in their hands, must have been a little astonished. While this was going on the Prince of Wales is said to have been off bird-nesting on Samson; but he was only six years old, and it was August! When the Prince visited Tresco in 1865, Augustus Smith himself drove the carriage. The Prince made a third visit to the islands in 1902, as King Edward VII.

Another Prince of Wales, the late Duke of Windsor, came by destroyer in 1921. In 1933 he arrived by Royal Air Force flying boat, and went back in the *Scillonian*. His father, King George V, is said to have visited the islands when a midshipman in the Royal Navy.

Since 1955, when the Duke of Edinburgh arrived by helicopter, there have been a series of royal visits by him, the Queen Mother, and the Queen herself, the islands making a break in the voyage of the royal yacht from the English Channel to Scottish waters for the autumn holiday at Balmoral. During Prince Charles's minority Queen Elizabeth presided over the Duchy Council and the visits of Prince Philip were very much business trips; with the aid of helicopters he has visited all the inhabited islands. When the Queen and the Duke came ashore in 1967 they had Prince Charles and Princess Anne with them; the first time that either had been taken on a royal tour. As the royal youngsters walked out of the Duchy Home Farm, then Trenoweth, Prince Charles said to his sister, 'Annie, you're having too much to say.' His sister, just seventeen, stopped in her tracks to reply, 'Mate, you should talk!' The prince's twenty-first birthday was marked by a house in the Garrison being set aside for him. Tamarisk, a two-bedroom house was built in 1966 and for a time occupied by the assistant to the Duchy land steward. Prince Charles first came privately for the weekend of 21–3 September 1973, flying from Culdrose in a helicopter of the Queen's Flight, fishing, visiting off-islands and farms on St Mary's, and walking the nature trail to Holy Vale.

VISITING SHIPS

Naval occasions have been frequent, from the famous frigate captain of Nelson's time, Admiral Pellew, who came ashore to a dance, down to Admiral Lord Fraser of North Cape, who came by destroyer in 1948 to stay at the Abbey. Battleships like the *Emperor of India*, *Marlborough* and *Rodney* came between the wars

Page 141 The packet boats: *(top)* the *Lady of the Isles* (in service 1875–1904); *(centre)* the *Lyonnesse* (1889–1917); *(bottom)* the *Scillonian* on the right (1956 – given three more years of life in 1974) with the *Queen of the Isles* (1965–70) on the day when the *Queen* first came into service. The two ships are alongside St Mary's Quay

Page 142 Air traffic: (*above*) a Rapide fixed wing aircraft at St Mary's Airport with the first helicopter to come into service, 1 May 1964; (*below*) a Short 184 seaplane taking off from the Road in 1917, one of the Royal Naval Air Service planes then based on Tresco

with their big crews; in 1953 the aircraft carriers *Indefatigable* and *Implacable* came on a 'jolly' with combined crews of 4,000 men. They sailed at the onset of a gale leaving men ashore; even more serious was the mountain of unconsumed food and drink the islanders had laid in. Another aircraft carrier, *Bulwark*, with a huge crew in 1956 let her men ashore in parties of 500, enough to cause congestion in Hugh Town. There were no shore visits when two Russian warships anchored in the Roads in 1963.

Passing Atlantic liners have always been familiar sights but the ships of the Holland-Amerika line from the 1920s onwards made a point of sailing close past the islands to give their passengers a good view. Cruise liners have also from time to time put from 100 to 150 passengers ashore on day visits; the Coast Line's *Southern Coast* in 1933 and since 1959 the Swedish *Kungsholm* and the Norwegian *Meteor* have done this on a number of visits. Tresco gardens have been their usual objective.

Up to 1912 paddle steamers from Plymouth and the Bristol Channel were visitors from time to time on excursion trips. These ended after the *Cambria* caught bad weather after leaving the islands and reached Plymouth 'looking as if she had gone through a gun battle'. The Campbell paddle steamer *Bristol Queen* resumed these calls after half a century with 100 passengers in 1963. But it was a short-lived revival and she went out of service in 1968. There was an odd visit of the *Balmoral* with 200 day passengers in 1972.

Yachts have changed since the great Victorian craft of the Duke of Leeds and the Duchess of Sutherland, or the square-riggers of Lords Runciman and Brassie, called at Scilly. Now ocean racers and little cruisers are commonplace all through the summer months. Even the famous Frenchman Eric Tabarly ran aground on Porth Cressa Brow in his first *Pen Duick* in 1959; he was very young. St Mary's Pool and New Grimsby Harbour are often crowded; on one evening in 1969 there were nineteen yachts anchored between Bryher and Tresco wearing British, French, Irish and German ensigns.

They have given little trouble; one fatal fire off New Grimsby, the occasional stranding in shallow water or broken spar is about all. Accidents to visitors generally are rare; just the odd broken leg or bathing incident. Sunburn is the commonest injury, helped by the clear air and fresh winds.

SIMPLE PLEASURES

Visitors no longer tour St Mary's in the town carrier's wagonette; they have buses, taxis, and can even hire bicycles. They have motor launches instead of sailing craft, though they can now hire sailing dinghies. But lazing on the beaches, swimming, walking, fishing, shrimping – 'the bracken on Samson . . . provides ample cover for those who are still in the romantic years', wrote J. N. McFarland Moyle in 1932 – these are still the island attractions. If visitors have any energy left in the evenings there are bars, restaurants, occasional film shows, coloured transparencies illustrating talks on the islands history instead of magic lantern shows, and the flash of the lighthouse across the sea.

Two little girls stopped the postman on Bryher one morning, where the sound of the lapping tide is never far away. They were carrying buckets and spades. 'Are we,' they asked, 'going the right way to the sea?'

9 COMMUNICATIONS

THE PACKET BOATS

THE need of Scilly for regular communication with the mainland increased all through the eighteenth century as the maritime importance of St Mary's developed. Open boats had provided the link, at four to six weeks intervals in summer and even longer gaps in winter, through the century. Sometimes it was worse; Borlase in 1752 remarked on 'seventeen weeks without any provisions whatsoever or intelligence'. The growth of shipping and the garrison in the wars with Revolutionary France sharpened the need; when the war was resumed in 1803 it was the garrison commander who recommended giving a mail contract to James Tregarthen, master of the 30-ton *Hope*.

Scilly had been held back by the slow development of roads in Cornwall. The first mail coach did not reach Truro until 1799 and the mail came on to Penzance by horse. Not until 1820 did the coaches reach Penzance. Tregarthen was required to sail from Penzance on Fridays, after he had personally collected the mail from the post office, and to return with the island mail on Sundays. He and his brother John operated the service until 1831, making a practice of reaching Penzance on Thursdays, market day there. In that year the *Cherub* was transferred to the St Mary's Shipping Company. When the *Cherub* was lost in 1837 the *Lord Wellington* was brought into service. Her master was Captain Frank Tregarthen, not closely related to his predecessors, who was to launch his hotel and command the islands' packet boats for the next thirty-six years.

The *Wellington* was a small ship, Tregarthen an individualist, and Augustus Smith had arrived with home county ideas. The Post Office and Mr Smith were soon complaining loudly; one

145

complaint was that the service ran to suit the company rather than the royal mail. Once Tregarthen was in sight of the Eastern Isles when he remembered he had left the mailbags in the Dolphin Hotel at Penzance, and had to turn back. There was much arguing about the contract. The company built a bigger ship, *Lioness*, but the Post Office refused the increased contract they had offered. Tregarthen refused to collect the mail from the Post Office. Two naval cutters were put in to carry the mail while *Lioness* went on with the market run, but by October the cutters were withdrawn; they found the winter weather too much and were costing the government ten times as much as the £100 contract the Post Office was refusing to pay. Then they tried giving a man 14s a week and his fare to sail as an ordinary passenger on the *Lioness*, carrying the mail secretly. 'The person sent with the mail arrived all well – though dreadfully ill' was the report. He was discovered, and barred from the ship. Finally the company was given the contract in 1848, at £150 a year, for a twice-weekly service, and three years later they replaced *Lioness* with *Ariadne*.

Coastal steamers on the Cork–London run had been passing the islands since 1823, and excursion steamers calling since 1831. The West Cornwall Railway line was approaching Penzance and in 1858 the St Mary's shipping agents, Buxton and Banfield, with other ship-owners and merchants, formed the Scilly Isles Steam Navigation Company. They chartered the paddler *Scotia* from the Kingston-Holyhead service and put her into service in 1858 while their own ship was completed at Renfrew. She was propelled by a single screw, quite advanced for her day. Brunel's *Great Western* was still the crack Atlantic ship and the Scillonians called their first steamer the *Little Western*. She came on station in December 1858, in time to meet the first trains of the West Cornwall Railway – an extension of the Great Western Railway – and launched a thrice-weekly service, on a mail contract of £300. A new era had begun for Scilly.

R. T. McMullen, who visited the islands in his yacht in 1861 and again in 1868, described in his book *Down Channel* the difference the railway and the steamships made. On his first visit the people of St Mary's were as Borlase had described them a century earlier; by 1868 all was changed. 'Chignons, crinolines, high-heeled boots and children's necklaces must be among the most important items of commerce. Then it was difficult to get meat, or anything but stale Penzance bread and butter: now plain provisions are as good as anywhere in the country.'

By 1870 there were demands on the mainland for a second ship in the service. The railway had vastly increased public mobility and the shareholders of the West Cornwall Railway bought the Clyde tourist paddle steamer, the *Earl of Arran*, in 1871 and put her into excursion runs to the islands from Penzance. Just a year later, while the *Little Western* was being repainted and the *Earl of Arran* acting as relief, she was cast away with 100 passengers on board. Captain Deason had let an unlicensed pilot, Stephen Woodcock, take her close under St Martin's 'to save twenty minutes' but she struck Irishman's Ledge and was only just beached close to Nornour. Her boiler is still there, exposed at low tides.

That was in July. In October the *Little Western* went to aid a disabled vessel but was beaten by another steamer. Coming back close under Samson she struck Southward Wells and became a total loss, though again without loss of life. It was the end of the Scilly Isles Steam Navigation Company. Augustus Smith had died that year, leaving little money and a young heir who had not yet resolved to take over his inheritance. The Hugh Town merchants were aware that shipbuilding was in decline, and fewer deep-sea vessels calling. Money was tight, and the future uncertain.

For the next forty-five years the island packet service was in the hands of the West Cornwall company. They used the paddler *Guide* and then the bigger paddler *Queen of the Bay*, built for pleasure work on the Lancashire coast, until their yacht-like *Lady of the Isles* could be completed at Hayle. She joined the *Queen* in 1875 and both operated until 1885, when the *Queen* was sold. The *Lady* was probably the best-loved ship ever in the service; she remained on the run until she struck rocks off Lamorna in 1904 and was declared a total loss. A Penzance salvage company bought her and got her back to work as a salvage vessel. She was still doing relief work on the Scilly run in 1935 – the oldest ship carrying Atlantic mail, it was said – and ended her honourable career on a mine outside Falmouth in 1940, sixty-five years old.

The West Cornwall had a second ship, *Lyonnesse*, built at Hayle, and brought her into joint service in 1889. She was a most distinctive ship, twice the size of the *Lady of the Isles* and with two funnels abeam, but she was always regarded as a bad sea boat. There is a legend of a day-tripper from St Austell moaning all through one crossing 'Throw me overboard; throw me overboard!' To replace the *Lady*, the West Cornwall company bought *Deerhound* in Blackpool in 1905. They had now been running two ships since 1875, with the exception of the four years between the *Queen*'s sale and the arrival of *Lyonnesse*. But the company was in financial trouble and in spite of selling *Deerhound* in 1907 (she ended her career on the Pacific coast of Canada in the 1950s) they went bankrupt the same year. John Banfield, then living at Penzance, bought the remaining ship, the *Lyonnesse*, and formed a new company under the old name.

World War I caused many interruptions to the service, but it was a bombshell to the islands when Banfield took the *Lyonnesse* out of service in 1917 and sold her. Ministry of Shipping craft kept the islands going until the final run-down of the service bases saw their withdrawal. Scilly had to find its own salvation and a committee was formed, of whom it was said later that they did not know where to look for a boat, or money. But a fund was set up, members went from door to door drumming up support, selling 5s shares, and £20,000 was raised in the islands; in March 1920 the Isles of Scilly Steamship Co Ltd was incorporated, and has been in business ever since. A former fishery protection vessel was bought from Admiralty Disposals, renamed *Peninnis*, and became the first island-owned packet for nearly half a century. But she was small and uncomfortable, and everyone was relieved when the company was strong enough to build the *Scillonian* which came into service in January 1926. She served for nearly thirty years, mostly with a Mousehole man, Captain Joe Reseigh in command, surviving two strandings and the perils of World War II.

A new *Scillonian* of 921 gross tons, twice the tonnage of her predecessor, and costing £250,000, came into service in March 1956. With her greater speed and comfort, and capacity for 600 passengers, she represented a great step forward. The company enjoyed 'wonderful years' in 1962 and 1963, cargoes were heavy and the demand was such that passengers were being left behind.

The steamship company confidently ordered a second, smaller steamer at a cost of £180,000, and *Queen of the Isles* came into service in April 1965. But between her ordering and launching British European Airways had replaced their fixed-wing air-craft service to the islands with helicopters. Where there had been too many passengers for one ship, now with helicopters lifting an average 500 passengers on peak Saturdays, there were not enough for two. The steamship company tried running their second ship on excursions from St Ives, then using her at week-ends and taking what charters came along, but the company was losing money. There were other problems: the building boom on St Mary's had ended, and a bad summer on top of national economic problems hit the holiday trade. Savings had to be found.

Since 1923 the steamship company had been running an inter-island launch service. They had started with the 16-ton launches *Ganilly* and *Gugh*, the latter being replaced in 1932 by the *Nor-nor* which had reached the island in World War I to serve the naval craft. She was condemned in 1948 and *Gugh* driven ashore in a winter gale in 1951. The company brought in 54ft naval heavy-duty launches, *Kittern* in 1949, *Tean* in 1953, and in 1961 a new *Gugh*. They carry the inter-island goods and some passengers all year round; in winter when the passenger launches are laid up they are the main links. But they have always been subsidised by the Penzance service; in 1965 they had cost the steamship company £11,000. The company did not want to sell its new ship, but had to make savings. The obvious cut was the launches. This brought a tremendous outcry. Islanders claimed that they had set up the company to benefit all islanders, that the directors had over-reached with their second ship.

In spring 1967 the company sold two passenger launches, *Gondolier* and *Lyonnesse*, and offered the rest of the launch fleet to anyone who would run it. There were no takers. Only one launch operated that summer, and finally an arrangement was found. An Off-Island Launch Service Committee was formed by the company and the Council of the Isles, the Ministry of Transport put up a subsidy of about £3,000, and with a small contribution from the rates (£320 in 1968) the service goes on. The steamship company found charter work for the *Queen of the Isles* for two years, and came back to two years of profit after two years of loss. But chartering was a makeshift, and in September 1970 the *Queen of the Isles* was sold; as the *Olohava* she now operates an inter-island service in the Friendly Isles, in the Pacific.

In 1972 the steamship company ordered a new ship to replace the ageing *Scillonian*, but the builders went bankrupt with the keel barely laid. The 1972 figure of £700,000 had risen to £2 million by 1974 and in August that year the company told shareholders that without government aid to build another ship they would end the service at the end of 1977, when *Scillonian* would have finished her economic life. After three winters relying on helicopters only during the steamer's refits, the islanders felt that their principal link with the mainland was in real danger.

AIR SERVICES

After Tresco's service as a seaplane base in World War I, flying boats made occasional visits in the 1920s. It was a plane belonging to the Prince of Wales which in March 1930 landed on the cricket field in Garrison, took off and then landed on the golf course. In October that year the islands played a part in the development of Atlantic air mails when the Canadian *Flying Leaf*, $23\frac{1}{2}$hr out from Newfoundland and losing oil pressure, sighted Tresco and landed on Pentle Beach. The crew, Erroll Boyd and Harry Connor, had to wait for fuel to be brought from RAF Mount Batten at Plymouth and carried up the beach in cans, before they could go on. During the next two or three years the German and French Atlantic liners were trying to speed mail deliveries by catapulting off planes between 300 and 500 miles west of Scilly. They became familiar sights to islanders in the 1930s and Cobham made plans for an air service. This did not materialise and on 15 September 1937 a service was started by Captain Olley's Channel Air Ferries. For a rental of £100 a year the golf club removed various hazards on the fifth and seventh fairways and this became the St Mary's terminal. The booking hut was near the second green, golfers had to clear the course when planes came in, and in windy weather helped by holding down the wings of the planes. St Just, near Land's End, was the mainland terminal, with a bus link to Penzance.

So well did the service operate that in 1938 the Duchy made room for an airport on the clifftops between Porth Hellick and Old Town. The runways, of which only a short strip has a surface to this day, point at the cliff and planes take off as if going over the bows of an aircraft carrier. It has been described as landing on an upturned saucer, or the roof of a house; daffodils were once grown in the fields and still appear in the grass.

The outbreak of war stopped the civilian service and the RAF took over the airfield. But a mail service was needed for the troops and was organised by Olley. His chief pilot, Captain Michael Hearn, who had started flying in 1919 and had opened the Scilly service, was released from the RAF in 1941 to restart the flights. Hearn did not retire from flying until 1962, the most celebrated pilot ever on the Scilly run. He brought in the DH89, the Rapide, which was to be the standard fixed-wing aircraft on the service for many years.

When civilian airlines were nationalised after the war the Rapides were repainted in the colours of British European Airways, who took over in 1947. Two years later some £15,000 was spent improving facilities; a control tower, first-aid post, office, waiting room and fire station were built, radio landing aids installed and radio contact established with the planes on the crossing. In 1953 the planes carried 18,900 passengers each way, and in 1957 it was said to be the hardest-worked domestic service in Britain with two pilots making eight take-offs every summer Saturday. In 1959, 29,100 passengers were carried.

Though the volume of air traffic was increasing, the Scilly landing field could not take planes larger than the Rapides. Helicopters had already used the islands, one delivering mail to the Sixth Frigate Squadron in the Roads in May 1954 and one bringing the Duke of Edinburgh for a visit in 1955. BEA bought two American Sikorsky S-61N machines, capable of carrying twenty-eight passengers at 140 knots, boat-hulled and with two engines each capable of supporting the aircraft. The service opened on 1 May 1964, and in September of that year the service was further improved with a specially built heliport within a mile of Penzance railway station. BEA carried 54,000 passengers in its first year, pretty well capacity, and by 1973 the annual figure was up to 68,248. Work began in June 1974 on a new terminal complex at St Mary's airport, costing £140,000.

There have been various private-enterprise rivals to BEA but none lasted long. Philip Cleife launched Mayflower Air Service from Plymouth in 1961 but the service ended when he was nearly killed taking off from St Mary's, with no passengers, in July 1963. When BEA switched to helicopters K. B. Neely bought the old Rapides and started Scillonian Airways. Captain Howard Fry started Westward Airlines in 1969; neither survives although Brymon Airways opened between Scilly, Newquay and Plymouth in 1972 and carried 3,781 passengers in their second year.

The route has a good record, with only one fatality when the pilot, Captain D. L. Distin, died after a St Just crash in fog in June 1938. Apart from Cleife's accident, St Mary's has only seen minor incidents.

The aircraft have carried freight as well as passengers. Since the winter of 1966 the helicopters have been modified in winter months so that they can carry up to 4,000lb in the flower season. At one point Lyonesse Growers arranged to move all its flowers by helicopter, with special flights as needed. Mail is also carried, BEA originally lifting it on alternate days when the steamers were not crossing. When first- and second-class mail was introduced, the first class began to be airlifted by early 1967, and second-class mail was going by air as well by the end of 1968.

POSTAL SERVICE

A post office was set up in Hugh Town in 1804 when the formal mail service began. It occupied various premises, notably what is now the Kavorna Café, then the home of a prim old couple, William Scadden and his sister Mary. A small window was opened when customers rang a bell and they transacted their business standing in the street. There was a posting slot under the window; when the steamer had sailed a notice 'Too Late' hung in the window. When the mail arrived another card 'Not sorted' hung there until the Scaddens were ready. He was also the island dentist, and would sit a patient on this office floor, grip the head between his knees, and heave with a ponderous old instrument until something gave way. Scilly rose to Crown Office standard and ceased to be a sub-post office of Penzance in 1897, when Algy Dorrien Smith had the present building erected, fitting the new local government dignity of the islands. The lumpy granite style of the Hugh Street post office can be seen in various Tresco buildings of the same period.

There were no country deliveries until 1880 and no country collections until the 1890s, but by 1930 there were posting boxes on St Mary's at Well Cross, Old Town, Parting Carn, Porthloo and the Quay, more following in the next couple of years at Lunnon and Telegraph. Hugh Town had a daily delivery of local mail by 1909 and the country a year or two later; since World War II and air services there has been a daily delivery of mainland mail as well.

Augustus Smith had to pay the Post Office £25 a year to get an office on Tresco, but it was not opened until 1868. St Martin's followed in 1879, Agnes in 1880, and Bryher in 1888. The off-island sub-postmaster, often the father figure of his island, originally had to collect the mail from St Mary's, using a sailing boat to collect the wicker hampers. Bryher collected from Tresco. Since the start of inter-island launches they have brought the mail from St Mary's to the various off-island landing points.

TELEGRAPHS AND TELEPHONES

Telegraph is a place name on St Mary's; it commemorates the fact that in 1814 semaphore arms were erected on the Corsican tower there and the islands were in communication with London through a series of such stations. The first submarine telegraph cable was laid between England and France in 1851 and various private companies developed the system in Britain. When the government began plans to take them over the compensation terms looked so rewarding that a host of companies was quickly formed. The Scilly Isles Cable Company of 1868 made its cable and engaged a steamer to lay from Land's End. Five miles off shore the cable came to an end but the engineer was not to be beaten; he snapped the cable, steamed on with a few hundred yards trailing astern, landed the end near Deep Point on St Mary's and by fiddling the morse key pretended to be in touch with Land's End. The company issued their certificate, but the government refused to take it over.

A genuine cable was laid the following year, with the original office in Scadden's post office. In 1875 it was moved to John Gibson's general store in Silver Street, where the now famous photographic business was already beginning. Eighteen-year-old Alexander, later the most renowned of all Gibsons, was the only operator. It was just before the *Schiller* wreck: the cable office was at work night and day for a fortnight when Alexander collapsed, to sleep for 30hr.

Both cable and company failed in 1877–8, but Algy Dorrien Smith came to the financial rescue and the cable was turned over to the Post Office. They laid a new cable from Porthcurno in 1886 and by 1893 inter-island cables were laid, St Mary's to Agnes, St Mary's to St Martin's and thence to Tresco and Bryher. Originally this was for coastguard purposes but in 1894 the off-island post offices were connected for public use.

The cable and its morse messages were the sole link with the mainland until 1938, when telephone connection was established through short-wave radio. The Scillonia exchange on St

Mary's gave limited facilities to the off-islands, which were limited to ten subscribers of whom only one could be linked with St Mary's at a time. An automatic exchange on Tresco served that island, Bryher and St Martin's from 1957, and in May 1968 all the islands went automatic on Subscriber Trunk Dialling with forty-eight channels on the radio link to the mainland. Three hundred simultaneous calls became possible after the microwave link of 1972. Odd that the radio link should have been effected so late, considering that Marconi conducted successful experiments from Telegraph in 1901 and the coastguard service set up an 180ft mast there the same year, moving their station to Telegraph at the same time.

RADIO AND TELEVISION

Radio programmes did not become generally available in the islands until after the opening of 5PY, the BBC station at Plymouth, in 1924. By the next year the islands were 'showing an increased interest in wireless reception', valve sets could be bought from A. H. W. Nance on the Parade, and there were sets on Agnes and Bryher before the end of the year. Next year Carn Thomas School was listening to Daventry and 2LO, the London station. By 1931 it was estimated that there were over 200 sets in the islands.

Again the islands had to wait for television. When the BBC erected the North Hessary mast on Dartmoor in 1956 sets began to appear in the islands, but the picture was not satisfactory. The combined ITV/BBC2 mast on Caradon Hill in East Cornwall gave a little improvement but no reception was really good until the BBC transmitter on Telegraph came into service in 1969, transmitting BBC1 and the radio programmes. BBC2, ITV and colour arrived in 1974. The mast is a dominant mark on the island skyline, and chimneypots sprout aerials as profusely as elsewhere.

NEWSPAPERS AND MAGAZINES

Newspapers reached the islands spasmodically in the last century. In 1854 a subscription newsroom where the papers could be read was opened in the old Custom House in Hugh Town; the interest in news was built up by the Crimean War. The Zulu War of 1879 sparked fresh interest and the newsroom took a special service of press telegrams. Central News supplied such telegrams in the South African War and World War I, and when various social institutes in Hugh Town amalgamated into the Scillonian Club the press telegram service continued there until 1930, when most people were getting their urgent news by radio.

The first daily newspapers to reach the islands on the day of publication were the *Western Morning News* and the *Western Daily Mercury*, both founded in Plymouth in 1860, but they could only reach Hugh Town on steamer days. The *Morning News* took over its rival in 1923 and since then, with the weekly *Cornishman*, founded in Penzance in 1878, has been the island Bible. But daily papers, either from London or Plymouth, on the day of publication were not really possible until the beginning of air services; now with the helicopter service it is usually possible to buy the day's paper in Hugh Street before the 10.15 pleasure launches leave. For a time specially chartered planes brought Sunday newspapers by noon; but for some years now the islands have had to wait till Monday morning for them.

Since March 1925 the islands have had their own quarterly magazine, *The Scillonian*. It was founded by the then chaplain, the Rev C. L. T. Barclay, and the headmaster, Mr Geoffrey Fyson, who had already had a volume of poetry published in London. When they left the island the new headmaster, Mr H. T. Ward, took over with issue No 15. Messrs William and Tregarthen Mumford became editors in March 1946 and Tregarthen's son Clive, a *Morning News*-trained newspaperman, became editor in 1967 with his father still handling distribution. From the second issue *The Scillonian* has carried on its cover a woodcut of a barque by Charlotte Dorrien Smith. The first print order was 600, a circulation of nearly 1,000 was reached by the 100th issue, and it still flourishes in spite of increasing costs; 1975 saw the 200th issue.

ROAD TRANSPORT

When Augustus Smith arrived in 1834 there were no metalled roads in the islands and only two horses on St Mary's. Donkeys with panniers and donkey carts were the main carriers. As late as 1950 an old man on Agnes could remember when that island had no horses, only donkeys or mules. The 'Scilly asses' were an early joke for comic postcards, and a bride left Agnes church in a donkey trap as recently as 1966.

One of Smith's first acts was to build roads, in the 1840s and 1850s. He dealt with St Mary's first, where the biggest problem was to cross the belt of sand between Hugh Town and the country. One can still find on the off-islands roads which are grassy tracks between hedges; not so long since all Scilly roads were like this. With roads came carts, and then the first spring carts reached St Mary's about 1870. By the end of the century fifty or sixty horses did all the farm and haulage work on St Mary's, but even wheelbarrows helped get flowers to the quayside. Hand barrows – handles at each end, and no wheel – can still be found in the islands.

A few bicycles had reached Scilly by the turn of the century, but it took World War I to bring a motor vehicle, in the shape of an RAF motor van operating between Porth Mellon and Holy Vale. E. N. Mumford was using a horse bus to take visitors to his Holgate's Hotel; inspired by the RAF he imported the chassis of a Ford car in 1920 and fitted the bus body to it. The first private car is claimed for 1918; by 1929 *The Scillonian* editor was writing 'the motor car has come to stay', and by 1933 the main road into Hugh Town had to be widened for the cars.

St Martin's had a lorry and a car by 1935, Agnes a 'Baby Austin' by 1936, and Bryher had to wait until 1945 for its first lorry. Only Tresco has set its face against motors; apart from the Dorrien Smith pony and trap, transport has to be by bicycle or tractor. Even holiday visitors and their luggage are collected from the landing places on a trailer with a central rack of seats and the Tresco Abbey nameplates from a former GWR locomotive. Tractors are still the commonest form of off-island transport.

St Mary's has much more sophistication. Vic Trenwith, the island entertainer on stage or off, met the first passenger plane in 1937 with a Willis bus built in Plymouth, and by the following year he had taxis as well. He and his nephew had three buses when Vic retired in 1970 (though he continued with taxis) and soon after a regular bus service began on St Mary's, operating a circular route from Hugh Town between 9am and 11pm.

The increased use of cars since the war in all the islands resulted from considerable road improvement schemes. Before World War II even the St Mary's roads outside Hugh Town were of waterbound stones. Wartime military traffic cut them up badly and a repair programme was launched in 1946. But because island motorists paid no road fund tax (their cars, unless bought second hand, were notable for blank number plates and no road fund discs), they paid nothing towards the roads. In 1947 the Council of the Isles proposed a voluntary tax, 10s a wheel for motor cycles and £1 a wheel for cars and lorries. Although the tax was more honoured in the breach than in the observance, the St Mary's roads were mainly tar-macadamed by 1951 and, though narrow and twisting, they have reasonable surfaces and families can even make Sunday afternoon drives around the few miles as they do on the mainland.

Agnes men were first to improve their roads; with a special 2s rate levy in 1954 they bought cement and, with all the island men giving a week's voluntary labour, aid from the council and a borrowed cement mixer, they completed their main road from Porth Conger to Periglis by 1965. With the Periglis slip improved by the islanders and the Porth Conger slip rebuilt (and its celebrated £6,000 lavatories), Agnes and its concrete highway set the pace for other islands. St Martin's men carried out a concreting programme in 1964–9, and Bryher began in 1967, though when they stopped for lunch on the first day with 40yd concreted up from the quay, a cow walked over their work leaving more than hoofprints! On Tresco Commander Tom improved the roads as part of his modernisation programme, with

Page 159 Inter-island launch service in wintertime: (*above*) loading flowers from Agnes and (*below*) St Martin's. Note the rough weather gear and the mixture of shore transport on St Martin's in these 1973 pictures

Page 160 (above) The Duke of Windsor (then Prince of Wales) leaving Star Castle. The islands are owned by the Duchy of Cornwall and the eldest son of the English Sovereign becomes Duke of Cornwall on birth; (below) a sub-tropical corner of Tresco Abbey Gardens, which Augustus Smith began in 1834 on a bare island without a tree on it. Seafaring Scillonians and plant-hunting members of the Dorrien Smith family since then have built up a collection of plants unique in Britain

a concrete highway from Appletree Bay to the Abbey Farm, and other roads macadamed.

St Mary's had road signs in 1944, driving tests in 1955, one-way traffic on St Mary's Quay in 1962 and yellow lines with 'No Parking' signs in Hugh Town by 1966. It was estimated then that the island had over 200 cars. The steamship company that year agreed not to bring in caravans; soon after they refused all cars between May and September, to stop visitors bringing them in.

But not since they were caught in the income tax net were islanders so incensed as in 1969, when the Vehicles and Driving Licences Act became law and Scillonians for the first time had to pay Road Fund Tax. It was argued that there were 400 cars in the islands, which would yield £8,000 a year tax, although St Mary's only had 11 miles of roads and petrol already cost up to 7d a gallon more than on the mainland because of freight charges. The tax became due on 1 April 1971, though to mark All Fool's Day perhaps it was held to apply only to residents of Hugh Town or those who took their cars into the town. This was because only the Hugh Town roads had been made over by the Duchy to the Council of the Isles and classified by Whitehall as principal roads, eligible for government grant. The other 9½ miles were private, because Duchy-owned. But within a year all St Mary's motorists were made liable, and in compensation there was a £100,000 road improvement scheme, three-quarters coming from the government, to widen roads and improve corners.

So the motor car age finally arrived, with SCY (a former Swansea registration) as the island letters. With driving tests, the breathalyser, MOT tests, and registration, the old days of un-numbered bangers with smooth tyres, doors tied with string or made of plywood, bodies covered with rust, came to an end. In early motoring days worn-out cars were pushed over a convenient cliff; later they were dumped in convenient corners, even behind the Town Hall, and forgotten. On the old twisting roads accidents were rare (a fatality unknown) and speed rarely over 25mph. Off-islanders are already frightened by the traffic on St Mary's.

HOUSES

STONE for walls, reeds for thatch; these must have been the traditional Scilly building materials from the beginning of time. But the wind is strong; Count Magliotti found the houses low, 'but in other respects resemble the buildings of England, being made of excellent material'. A few were slate-roofed, 'the more common ones have a peculiar sort of covering by way of roof, having nothing but a simple mat spread over the rafters, drawn tight all round'. Until the last century houses in exposed positions had their thatch secured with straw ropes, the plaiting of which was an Old Town industry. The housing supply seems to have been adequate; in 1790 people were housed right through the group at about five to a house, a reasonable family figure. Half the population then was on St Mary's, and half those people in Hugh Town, a figure that seems to have held good since the drift from Old Town to live in the shadow of Star Castle in the seventeenth century. Hugh Town grew with the expansion of the Napoleonic Wars; there were no houses past the Parade before the mid-eighteenth century but by 1822 the row of cottages facing the harbour reached out to Carn Thomas. The town spread out slowly during the nineteenth century towards what is now the Chaplaincy, but up to the end of World War I Hugh Street was still a straggle of irregular and old thatched cottages, some housing several families. The Duchy then rebuilt the street in its present monotonous shape, and added Longstone and Porthloo Terraces in the country. There too a number of farmhouses were rebuilt in the first quarter of this century, in the new flower prosperity.

The next spate of building came after World War II, with a

council estate of twenty-four houses going up at Porth Cressa on
2½ acres leased from the Duchy. The estate was designed by
Geoffrey Bazeley of Penzance to straggle up the hillside with
ordinary, bright-coloured cottages, and on completion in 1951
won an award from the Ministry of Housing and Local Government. Private bungalows were also going up; the cement blocks
either coming in by the *Scillonian* or being made in a plant at
Bant's Carn, north of Telegraph.

A new release of land by the Duchy in the late 1950s brought
another boom, with houses going up by the hospital, bigger ones
on the Garrison. In 1963 private blocks of flats were going up in
Hugh Town, facing the harbour, and the Council of the Isles
and the Duchy combined to tackle the housing problem. A 2-acre
estate of twenty-six houses began to go up at Old Town, to house
people employed in the essential services of the island and retired
Duchy tenants; a private housing estate was also started there. A
Plymouth contractor set up a hutted camp at Porth Mellon to
house his workmen; the presence that winter of so many un-
attached men made the Mermaid bar look like the Yukon gold
rush! Apart from the houses a new school at Carn Thomas and
sea defences at Old Town were in hand. In 1965 four firms of
builders had men on the islands.

The boom ended in 1966 when the Council of the Isles switched
from contract building to direct labour, taking over construction
of flats, a new museum, school extensions and an old people's
home. Costs were reduced, but the freight charges on bringing
materials to the islands added over £300 to the cost of each house.
Not all the new houses were objects of beauty, but the flats overlooking St Mary's Pool toned in well, and the accommodation for
old people overlooking the park meant that for the first time they
did not have to be removed to the mainland in their old age, cut
off from relatives and friends and familiar scenes.

On the off-islands the Tresco estate company, with direct
labour, developed a programme of modernising their cottages
through the 1960s, and on St Martin's Mr Dallimore built a
house for himself and three new cottages for his workpeople, and
modernised others. On Bryher the houses on Pool Green were re-

built in 1950 and the old coastguard houses renovated in 1959. Generally the Duchy was slower than either the Council of the Isles or lessees like Commander Dorrien Smith and Mr Dallimore to improve conditions. Dwindling populations in the off-islands reduced the housing demand. The sharp climb in house values was most felt in Hugh Town: in 1966 a 'luxury bungalow residence' was for sale at £18,000, in 1967 a terraced cottage in the Strand fetched £5,000 and in 1968 a one-bedroom flat overlooking St Mary's Harbour was withdrawn from auction when its reserve price of £8,500 was not reached. In Autumn 1973 'offers over £15,000' were sought for a three-bedroom bungalow in Hugh Town and a year later the agents were asking £30,000 for four-bedroom accommodation in the town.

DOMESTIC SERVICES

Wells have always been the water source of the islands, augmented by rain water from the roofs when not too polluted by seagulls. Increased modern demands have seen many new wells sunk in the twentieth century on all islands. Since the middle-1950s Hugh Town has had piped water from reservoirs on Buzza Hill and Garrison to which well water is pumped and by 1955 only ninety-seven houses of the 528 on St Mary's were without piped water but over a third were without water closets. The Duchy put mains sewerage into Hugh Town in 1938; outside the town cesspits have gradually replaced earth closets. All Tresco had piped water by 1969, and that year water mains were laid on Bryher. St Martin's and Agnes remained without any mains facilities, though a sewerage scheme for St Martin's was prepared in 1974. As it would cost £37,000 for a population of ninety-five its execution looked remote.

Seaside communities have commonly used the beach and the tides to remove their rubbish. Collections started on St Mary's after World War I with a tip on Porth Minick, east of Tolman Point, replaced by another on Lower Moor, on the country side of Hugh Town. Complaints of the burning led to the installation of an incinerator there by the Council of the Isles in 1969, but that was soon under pressure. On the off-islands the disposal of rubbish is largely a private matter still.

HEALTH SERVICES

When Heath arrived in 1750 he found no doctors, only a 'society of skilful aunts' who cured with simples and herbs and what medical supplies they got from visiting ships' doctors; they were midwives, dentists, everything. The occasional garrison surgeon was the only help. The great medical figure of the nineteenth century was Dr J. G. Moyle, 'who drew teeth at a shilling each and ushered many splendid Scillonians into the world at five shillings apiece'; he had to fix broken legs without anaesthetics while friends sat on the patient's head. Dr W. B. Addison (in practice 1912–27) used his own boat in fine weather with his wife as crew; in bad weather the gigs would fetch him as they had Dr Moyle. A boat to a Scilly doctor is as a car to one on the mainland; little wonder that Dr Moyle's son Trevellick, Dr Addison and one of his successors, Dr W. D. Bell, were all secretaries of the lifeboat.

An influenza epidemic which swept the islands in January 1892 and put not only the doctor but virtually the whole islands into bed at one time led to the formation of a Nursing Association which set up two district nurses on St Mary's and Tresco respectively to supplement the doctor's work; it was a memorial to Mrs T. A. Dorrien Smith who died in the outbreak. Its money-raising activities, notably the annual fête, became as much part of island life as the nurses' clinics, and in 1938 when an emergency hospital was built on St Mary's, on the hill between Hugh Town and Old Town, the Association lent £1,000. Another £5,000 was given by Mr W. G. K. Birkinshaw, a Wolverhampton business-man who had originated the En Tout Cas tennis courts. He and his wife settled at Seaways on St Mary's in 1920 and built it up as a model flower farm. All hospital cases had previously to go to Penzance.

The introduction of the National Health Service in 1948 brought many improvements to island facilities. By 1950 there were two resident doctors and the first resident dentist for whom a house was found on the Parson's Field council estate. Special hospital cases were still sent to the mainland, but six specialists attended the island hospital. In 1953 health clinics were opened on St Martin's and Agnes, in addition to the long-established district nurses' cottage on Tresco, now attended weekly by a nurse from St Mary's. The hospital was extended in 1965 and though there were spells when Dr Bell worked single-handed and under great pressure, that was remedied and with a pocket two-way radio linking him and the nurses always with the hospital, the islands were better served than ever before. In 1972 it was decided that a special launch should be available for the doctors and they now have the smart *Saint Warna*, operated by the Medical Launch Trust.

LIGHTING AND FUEL

A Tonic Solfa Glee Club made enough money from a concert in the infants' schoolroom in 1883 to give Hugh Town its first street lights. The jubilee was celebrated in 1933 by the installation of twenty-one electric lights through the town. This had been made possible by the formation in 1931 of the St Mary's Electricity Supply Co Ltd, which built a power station in Worsall's Quarry, off Church Road. In 1957 the South Western Electricity Board took over, their avowed aim to supply all the islands and at the same charge as the mainland. The off-islands still defeat them, and in 1969 householders on St Mary's were paying 2·5d a unit compared with 1·9d in Cornwall. But the board did start covering St Mary's at once; within three years they had 517 consumers and had to bring in a new generator. In 1966 a landing craft deposited a new 924kW diesel generator at Rechabite Slip and crowds watched its transfer to the quarry. Even that was a temporary measure; the board planned a new power station at Parting Carn and warned that supplies for St Mary's alone would cost between £200,000 and £400,000 in the next fifteen years.

On Tresco the estate company set up its own generator, at the back of the home farm, and linked up all the island. People on the other off-islands had to set up their own generators too; Bryher and Agnes both began in 1945 and St Martin's followed; since then the sound of the off-islands after dark is that of innumerable small generators running, as if so many two-stroke motor cycles were abroad.

WESTMINSTER AND WHITEHALL

'The islands have only three links with the mainland', Alec Beechman, sometime MP for St Ives, once said, 'me, the Bishop, and the asylum at Bodmin.' When Scillonians first voted is uncertain and probably less than a century ago. The Reform Act of 1832 did put the islands in the Western Division of Cornwall but few islanders could have qualified for a vote. Not until 1872 was St Mary's recognised as a polling station, and the political life of the islands probably starts with its inclusion in the St Ives Division when the Cornish constituencies were changed in 1885.

Certainly in modern times candidates at election times have held at least one meeting in Hugh Town, and there are branches of both Conservative and Labour parties (founded 1953) there.

From 1952 to 1968 there was a government office in Hugh Town dealing with sickness benefits, social security, unemployment benefits, passports, and other government business. Although unemployment reached the figure of forty-five in mid-December 1968 the office was closed and an officer came over once a week from Penzance to handle all the business; lack of need was given as the reason. The unemployment was mainly among hotel workers and also a result of the rundown of the building programme; but it was said that until a year or two before it had been rare for islanders to register as unemployed, even if seasonably out of work. In March 1973 only eleven men and seven women were registered as unemployed. In 1973 a small government office was opened off Porthcressa Road, attended by a Department of Employment officer for 4hr on Tuesdays, and the Ministry of Social Security on the other weekday mornings.

POLICE AND FIRE SERVICES

Scilly has long had a reputation for being law-abiding; a visitor in the 1850s said the islanders were 'extremely honest. In all my dealing with them I have never met with one attempt at fraud. They leave doors unbarred and linen on the hills to bleach, and young girls can walk about at any hour in safety.' Each parish vestry used to elect its constable annually, as it did church-wardens, but after a spell of drunkenness and fighting among visiting seamen, the constable of St Mary's was given a uniform in 1861, a small wage, and required to patrol the streets and see that the public houses shut at 11pm. Licensing hours came with the 1872 Licensing Act, and with the formation of the Council of the Isles in 1892 a Joint Police Committee was set up of the council and the magistrates. This body amalgamated with the Cornish Constabulary, which supplied first one and then two constables, based on the police house on the Parade with its cell at the back. With the regionalisation of police forces Scilly came under the Devon and Cornwall combined police authority and in 1974 had a sergeant and two constables, and a specially built police station in Hugh Town. A month before the station opened the island trio was augmented by an inspector and two constables from Penzance for a midnight raid on the Mermaid. The licensee and eleven islanders were fined; a man from St Martin's got off. Island reaction ranged from shock to loud laughter.

The seven magistrates meet in the Town Hall when there are cases to hear, which is not often; minor traffic offences, visiting drunks, shooting at protected birds and so forth make up the rare charge sheets.

Scilly has been remarkably free from serious fires, though both Holy Vale and Mount Todden were burnt down in the eighteenth century, and one side of Hugh Street destroyed by a fire which spread from the hearth of a woman baking bread. The only fatality of modern times was in a 1944 fire at Borough, Tresco. Until the late 1930s only bucket chains and extinguishers were available, though there had been calls for a voluntary brigade after a store fire in Hugh Town in 1930. When the war brought German incendiary bombs, two Auxiliary Fire Service crews came over from Penzance and trained local men; by that time the new Hugh Town water supply did yield eight hydrants.

When the National Fire Service reverted to local control in 1948 the Council of the Isles became a fire authority, the smallest in Britain and without any professionals. The late Alderman Cyril Short retired in 1970 from the post of Chief Fire Officer – the only volunteer of that rank in Britain – and recalled that when he took over in 1948 he had an ancient fire tender towed by a 1927 car, no escape ladders, and no pumps of any power. In time he was set up with a modern fire tender and, with another at the airport and co-operation with the fire brigade there, St Mary's was well covered. The volunteer force of twelve has a station at the east end of Porth Cressa.

On the off-islands heath fires have always been a problem. After a house was burnt down on Bryher in 1955 which meant a fire engine being taken across from St Mary's, each island was supplied with modern portable fire-fighting equipment and volunteer teams trained. Tresco and St Martin's have motorised units.

MUSEUM AND LIBRARY

The earliest museum in Scilly was that created by Alexander Gibson, the photographer, guide book writer and eccentric, in his shop in Church Street in 1933, an old-fashioned and unconnected display. The prehistoric finds on the Porth Cressa council house site after the war led to the formation of a Museum Association and eventually a museum was opened, largely based on the private collection of Mr R. M. Stephenson, then Clerk to the Council. After various homes, and the spurt given by new finds at Nornour and the interest stirred by visiting archaeologists, the council decided in 1964 to build a permanent museum, with flats above, on the site of the school canteen and old Rechabite Hall in Church Street, to be rented to and equipped by the Museum Association. The South West Area Museums Council helped with the display.

Within a month of the opening, on 15 July 1967, it was visited by the Queen, the Duke of Edinburgh, the Prince of Wales and Princess Anne. By 1973 it was attracting over 19,000 visitors a year; if they followed the displays in order from the entrance they received an admirable and well-illustrated account of the islands' history and life. The Museum Association has also produced a fine series of island monographs and built up a good library. A pioneer in its creation was Mrs Mary Mackenzie who made the original Nornour finds; unfortunately she died within two years of the opening. A 'fairy godfather' of the museum was Mr Kenneth Leach, a Wolverhampton businessman who spends a quarter of each year at his house, White Horses, on the Garrison. Since the opening the museum has been given the Gibson collection.

A branch of Cornwall County Library was opened in Hugh Town with 500 books in 1940; when it was moved into the new school in 1967 there were 2,000 books, with a constant turn-over of new titles.

SHOPS AND PASTIMES

In Hugh Town there has been a pharmacy since 1890 and shops of every description have spread through the town since the 1920s. Prices are higher than on the mainland because of freight charges; fish, oddly enough, is scarce because what is caught locally tends to go to Penzance buyers, and laundry is dear because all has to be sent to the mainland. Haircutting has been a problem at times, with the men going to the club steward or the women's shop (and being refused for a week before the Queen's visit in 1967 because so many women were having their hair 'permed'). But by 1974 there were two hairdressers, one with a sauna bath as well. Even a piano tuner makes regular visits; in 1959 he observed that there were more pianos in Scilly than in all the rest of his Cornish district.

Customs have changed as in most English rural areas. Nickla Thies, when neighbours spent all night eating, drinking, and dancing together after bringing in the corn, has given way to the church harvest festivals. Guise dancing at Christmas, a cross between folk dancing and Scottish first-footing at the new year, survived on Agnes up to 1939 and on St Martin's after the war; it was accompanied by practical jokes which have come to life again in Hugh Town on recent New Year's Eves. The tall maypoles on the Parade and the tar barrels rolled through the streets on Midsummer Night died with the shipyards. But since 1880 St Mary's has crowned its Queen of the May on May day on the Parade, and off-island schools have similar celebrations. The last century benefit society with its parade on the annual feast day behind St Mary's brass band has gone. The band survived until 1939 but the days when it entertained round the town on Saturday nights have long passed. The Rechabites had a band too; now there are pop groups. The annual carnival still flourishes.

SPORT

Cricket could have been described as the traditional game of the islands since its introduction by Augustus Smith, and inter-island matches were most popular. At the height of enthusiasm St Mary's had two teams, St Mary's (town) and Lyonesse (country), sharing pitches on Garrison where the Duchy opened a games pavilion in 1925. As off-island populations dwindled so cricket fell away. Association football has become the main team game, as on the mainland, though the two teams, Rovers and Rangers, are both St Mary's based. There is tennis on the Garrison. At various times both Bryher and Agnes have had courts.

The main inter-island sport nowadays is gig racing. Sailing races between the old pilot cutters gave way with their disappearance to racing between specially built craft, and with only a few breaks this century has seen regular sailing events. The Scillonian Sailing Club was formed in 1946; the headquarters were moved from Town Beach to Porth Mellon in 1968, with a Duchy-provided concrete slipway across the sand.

The most solidly based sport on St Mary's is golf. The club was founded by Dr Brushfield in 1904 on a nine-hole course, said to be the only one in Britain from which the sea can be seen from every hole; the view itself is a hazard. The first pavilion was opened in 1935. After the war the course was steadily improved and membership grew until in July 1969 a new £10,000 clubhouse given by the Duchy was opened. With its bar and lounge it has made a considerable improvement to the social amenities of St Mary's, both for islanders and visitors. In 1973, with 250 resident members, and with the acquisition of another 10 acres, the nine holes were redesigned and extended.

CLUBS AND SOCIETIES

In Hugh Town the main social centre is the Scillonian Club, founded in 1921 by the amalgamation of the newsroom, billiard club and United Services club. With the Duchy sale of Hugh Town property the club bought their premises in 1949 and acquired a licence in 1951, whereupon membership rose from sixty-four to 230. In 1965 the Prime Minister, Harold Wilson, opened a new bar overlooking the harbour; 'Unaccustomed as I am to public speaking', he began.

Hugh Town had its first lodge of Freemasons in 1756, formed by the Collector of Customs, Isaac Head, who had been appointed by the Grand Lodge of England as Provincial Grand Master of the Province of the Isles of Scilly and the Adjacent Isles. He was the first master of Lodge Dolphin (no 365), reformed as Lodge Godolphin (no 281) in 1783. Its members seem to have been mainly drawn from non-islanders, though a few pilots were members. Its strength diminished after the arrival of Augustus Smith, though he was a Freemason and later Provincial Grand Master of Cornwall. The lodge was erased in 1851. After the reforming in 1961 of Lodge Godolphin (no 7790) the original jewels were found in Tresco Abbey.

The Independent Order of Rechabites, a friendly society based on total abstinence, was strong in the last century. St Mary's has had a Women's Institute since 1954 (the first talk was on income tax) and Agnes started an institute that year too. Girl Guides and Brownies have flourished since 1929. Scouts have had a more chequered time. But organisations flourish far more strongly than in a mainland town of comparable size; the *Scillonian* records the activities of the Chamber of Commerce (founded 1966), Hotel and Guest House Association, Army Cadets (1971), Ladies Life-boat Guild, Dancing School, Bridge Club, Rotary Club (1971) and Inner Wheel (1972), Round Table, Theatre Club (1967), Scillonian Entertainers (1951), Stamp Club, pre-school play-group, Gourmets' Society, Pony Club, Folk Club, British Legion, Music Society, Judo Club, Toc H (1957) and Buffaloes (1974).

CINEMA

The island's first cinematograph show was in the Town Hall in 1898. Bertie Ashford, island barber and Methodist organist, began film shows in the Bible Christian Hall in 1927. The arrival of the electricity company made talking films possible and the first was *Rome Express*, shown in 1934 by Mr Ashford in the Atlantic Hotel in January of that year. In partnership with Harold Solomon he took over the old Wesleyan Sunday School in Garrison Lane, made redundant by the union of the Methodist Churches, and installed 16mm talking cinema projectors. There were major improvements in 1943 and notably in 1950 when the building was reopened as the Plaza. The two families almost ran the cinema by themselves, but in 1963 it closed its doors under the impact of television. It was revived the following year, only to close again early in 1973. It had a steady rival for twenty years in shows of colour slides on island life and history given variously in the Town Hall and the Church Hall, in aid of church and lifeboat funds. The shows still take place.

Amateur theatre performances and concert parties have long been popular, notably since the formation of the Scillonian Entertainers led by Mrs Hilda Pearce and Vic Trenwith. But small professional repertory companies sometimes appear, even taking Shakespeare to the off-islands, and the first circus for thirty-six years, that of Winship and Son, appeared in St Mary's in 1964.

SOCIAL LIFE

Self-entertainment is the key to off-island life, inevitably, with the Reading Room in each case the social centre. Whist drives

and dances are held in them, Christmas parties, wedding receptions and from time to time amateur theatricals. In 1925 the
Tresco Reading Room (the former Baptist Chapel) was having
film shows and has progressed to talkies. St Martin's Reading
Room was built by islanders in 1932. Agnes added a billiard room
to the Reading Room (the former Bible Christian Chapel) in
1938, with a table given by Lord Cranley (later the sixth Viscount
Onslow). One might argue that the people of Scilly are as well off
as those of any rural English area. Few towns the size of Hugh
Town have so many facilities, or such choice of activities, largely
because Scillonians cannot easily go to another town and so have
to set them up themselves. The off-islands are in theory no worse
off than many English villages, with a social life revolving round
one general shop, church, pub (at long last on all the islands save
Bryher, whose people can easily get to Tresco) and village hall
(reading room in island terminology). Only the few youngsters
on the off-islands will bother with a night boat trip for an evening
in Hugh Town. In some ways the isolation helps because both
off-island and Hugh Town people have to look inwards, to
themselves, instead of to the nearest city.

But the English villager, or market town resident, can get to
the nearest city by stepping into a car; he does not have to book
seats on a helicopter, or spend 3hr each way on a steamer. He can
go at the drop of a hat in most cases. It is not that people want to
do this often, but the consciousness that one can escape defeats the
claustrophobic feeling. 'And who wants to buy a dress that has
been in a Hugh Town shop window for a week', as an island
woman once said.

11   CHURCHES AND EDUCATION

SOON after the Godolphins regained their lord proprietorship of the islands at the Restoration in 1660, they rebuilt
the church at Old Town, the nave in 1666, a north aisle and
galleries in 1669, and a south aisle in 1677. Yet the population
was already moving from Old Town to Hugh Town. The first
chaplain, so-called because it was a personal, household appointment by the lord proprietor, was appointed in 1669. He and his
successors took over without institution or induction, and certainly by the mid-eighteenth century was concentrating his
attentions on St Mary's with the exception of an Easter sermon
on Tresco.

There were various buildings used for worship on Tresco,
Bryher, Agnes and St Martin's rebuilt and repaired over the
years, and on these islands the agent appointed a fisherman to
read prayers and preach 'according to the doctrines of the Church
of England. They are men chosen for their exemplary morals, and
no ill grace to the pulpit'. Whether this could be said of the chaplains of the eighteenth century, a time when the Church of
England was not noted for its zeal, is another matter. Heath in
1750 said priests who took the chaplaincy had failed to find pre-
ferment elsewhere, not an encouraging statement, and one at
least seems to have dabbled in smuggling.

The islands were outside the jurisdiction of any Anglican
bishop, and in 1752 a Shropshire rector gave £250 to the Society
for the Promotion of Christian Knowledge in Foreign Places for
religious and secular education on Tresco. The society, founded
in 1698 and concerned largely with the American colonies, was
involved in the Isle of Man and later in the Channel Islands, but

the position in Scilly became unique in that from the educational start the society became involved in a 'mission' and the support of 'missionaries' in a part of the British Isles. The first missioner arrived in 1775; the second, the Rev John Troutbeck, jumped into the chaplaincy when it fell vacant in 1780, and then continually quarrelled with the third missioner, one reason for a visit by the SPCK president to the islands in 1786. A second SPCK missioner later was established on Agnes.

Just before Augustus Smith arrived in Scilly, Henry Philpotts was appointed Bishop of Exeter, whose see then embraced all Cornwall. Like Smith, the new bishop was autocratic, reforming and energetic. He visited the islands in 1832, in his first year of office, the first recorded visit ever of a bishop, and confirmed 239 people, some very old. One wonders how things were managed before his time, for Anglicans can only receive communion after confirmation by a bishop. Philpotts found the centre of population to be in Hugh Town, and its church over the hill at Old Town in sad repair. No doubt it was Bishop Philpotts who prompted the building of a new church at Hugh Town, and persuaded King William IV to pay for it. But King William did nothing until Smith took over the lease of the islands in 1834; one of the terms was that Smith should build the church and its cost was extracted from the money Smith paid for the lease; he also agreed to pay the stipends for the island clergy. Smith himself designed the church, with its galleries rising up each side from the floor of the nave and its tall narrow windows, and the bishop came in 1838 to consecrate it and make more confirmations.

An Order in Council that year made the islands part of the Diocese of Exeter. Philpotts then refused to recognise the SPCK missionaries unless they became curates of the chaplain. The society has never maintained clergy in an English diocese and so in 1840 they bowed out, endowing the off-island clergy with a grant of £4,000 and pensioning off their two missionaries. The chaplains lived for some time on the site of the present Bishop and Wolf public house; when the governorship ended the house next to the church, which had latterly been their residence, became the chaplaincy.

Since the 1820s there has been a resident priest on Tresco and for a time, after Smith enlarged the old cottage-church, a separate conventional district was formed of Tresco and Bryher. The present Tresco church was built as a monument to Augustus Smith by Lady Sophia Tower. It was dedicated in 1882 by the first Bishop of Truro, a see carved from Exeter a few years earlier, and which has since had the oversight of the islands. The conventional district was dissolved in 1963 and became again part of the parish of Scilly, with the Tresco priest as the chaplain's curate. Commander Dorrien Smith surrendered a patch of land which the Duchy then gave to the Church Commissioners, where a new parsonage was built on funds raised by a £6,000 appeal. Later the curate's title was changed to assistant priest; in June 1974 he became Team Vicar of Tresco, Bryher and St Martin's, within the Scilly parish of which the chaplain remained rector. Until 1959 there were intermittently resident priests, commonly in semi-retirement, on both Agnes and St Martin's. In 1960 the Duchy gave a motor boat to the chaplain to enable him to tend his scattered flock, and the priest of Tresco also has his boat. It is commonplace for them to go to church in cassock and oilskins, and lay readers support them. The present church on Bryher was built in 1742, rebuilt and enlarged in 1822. The churches on St Martin's and Agnes both date from about 1845, in the building years of Augustus Smith.

Services are still held from time to time at Old Town Church and its churchyard is still the burial ground for St Mary's. Few churches have a more beautiful or peaceful setting.

THE METHODISTS

John Wesley made a rough crossing to Scilly in September 1742 and preached twice in the street of Hugh Town, but he found the islands 'a barren dreary place'. He never returned. It was the Wesleyan Minister of St Ives, the Rev Joseph Sutcliffe, feeling 'he was to travail for the souls of the smugglers', who crossed in 1788, and a Wesleyan Society was formed on St Mary's with a church in Garrison Lane. The society flourished, adding chapels

L

at Holy Vale in 1815, Old Town in 1819, Tresco in 1820 and rebuilding the Garrison Lane Church in 1825–8.

But in 1821 the Bible Christians, a Cornish break-away movement from the Wesleyans with a more primitive approach, were moved by the national appeals for the off-islands in their distress to send a young missionary, Mary Anne Wherry. Among her many converts was William Gibson of St Martin's 'who gave up the contraband trade and . . . became a burning and shining light'. By 1832 they had chapels in Hugh Town and on St Martin's and Agnes, with three resident ministers. In 1836–7 they built their church in Church Street, rebuilt again in 1900. Indeed they flourished with the Methodists through the nineteenth century, in spite of a clause in the original Duke of Leeds's leases that the free churches should not hold services at the same time as the Anglicans. It was common for Methodists of both sects on St Mary's to attend their service first and then go to the parish church. In 1851 there were five Anglican churches in the islands with 1,274 seats, three Wesleyans with 734 and four Bible Christian with 515 – 20 more Anglican seats than Methodist. A French traveller in 1860 wrote that 'the religious movement is dominated by dissenting sects and the Ranters have lately produced a real reformation in morals'.

A national merger in 1907 made the Bible Christians into United Methodists, who in turn amalgamated nationally with the Wesleyans in 1932 to become the Methodist Church. The Scilly Union came in 1934 and eventually established itself in the former Bible Christian Church, where the Methodists still worship. St Martin's alone of the off-islands still has a Methodist church in the care of local preachers and the St Mary's minister since the last resident minister in the 1950s.

THE BAPTISTS

Close behind the Wesleyans the Baptists arrived in the islands; indeed the Rev G. C. Smith of Penzance who first visited Scilly in 1814 was the main agent in calling national attention to the distress of the off-islands. The Baptist Itinerant Aid Society established Scilly as their first missionary station and their first minister was Smith's assistant, the Rev J. T. Jeffery. They established chapels on the Strand in Hugh Town, at Maypole, and on all the inhabited off-islands, including Samson. Augustus Smith was no narrow churchman but he eventually fell out with the Baptists and in 1843, in the words of the General Baptist Repository, he 'caused notice to be served at the chapels'. They were all closed but the faith lingered on Bryher. A new Baptist chapel was built there in 1874 and it continued for nearly a century before the congregation died out. In 1972 it was converted into a private house.

ROMAN CATHOLICS

The Roman Catholic Church returned to Scilly when the Canons Regular of the Lateran from Bodmin Priory took over a building in the Strand which Augustus Smith had built as a girl's school in 1860. Father McElroy conducted the first service in August 1930 in the Church of St Mary Star of the Sea (one of the Virgin's titles). Count Leoni was one of the prime movers in its establishment; Father Doran in 1947 was the first resident priest.

The days when the Anglicans were alarmed by the 'sectaries' and the 'Ranters' have gone; today the ecumenical spirit is as strong in Scilly as elsewhere. There are united services, and helpful friendships between the denominations.

EARLY EDUCATION

Godolphin set up charity schools in the islands in 1747; the first interest of the SPCK was educational and the society established schools in the six then inhabited islands by 1774. They were little better than dame schools, with mainly aged teachers, although there was a Duke of Leeds School in Hugh Town whose master was of enough education to be clerk to the Council of Twelve and in 1808 the SPCK missioner on Agnes.

But education was a hobby horse of Augustus Smith. After the SPCK departure he built new schools on all the islands, compelled attendance through his authority as landlord, and was not above appearing in the schools and taking over instruction himself. A government inspector in 1848 said nearly all the children from the age of two to thirteen were receiving instruction, reading and writing well, having some knowledge of history, geography, grammar and arithmetic. The older boys were taught navigation, there were night schools for them too, and it was a Scilly boast that all the lads who went to sea became masters or mates. In 1851 there were ten schools with 755 pupils and Smith made attendance compulsory in 1856, charging parents 1d a week for the privilege but 2d a week for children who stayed home. In Hugh Town he built a new infants' school (now the Church Hall) and a girl's school behind in the Strand; the boys stayed at Carn Thomas which was enlarged in 1870. The Education Act of that year, meant to supplement the provision of schools, did not affect the islands which had long anticipated its requirements of education for all.

EDUCATION SINCE 1890

With the Education Act of 1902 the Council of the Isles became the local education authority. Carn Thomas remained a controlled Church of England School, as it still is, but was considerably enlarged and took back the infant and girls' departments in 1906. As the one school on St Mary's attended by all the children on the island – as on the off-islands – it has helped build the almost classless society that so marks Scilly. Perched on a bluff above Porth Mellon with the beach serving as a playground extension, at the meeting point of Hugh Town, the harbour, and the countryside, it is small wonder that the school, and its generations of devoted teachers, has a special place in island affection.

This affection, and the cost of education to a small authority, has produced the endless battles that followed the Butler Education Act of 1944. Children of grammar school standard were boarded on the mainland, at the expense of the Council of the Isles. Secondary education for all, which the new Act required, meant building a second school on St Mary's or sending all over-twelves to the mainland. Already primary education was costing Scilly £41 a child a year compared to £28 in Cornwall; and grammar school education £210 a child compared with £54 in Cornwall.

By 1950 it had been resolved to modernise the off-island schools and Carn Thomas for primary education, build a new secondary modern school and a hostel for off-island over-twelves in Hugh Town, and continue sending grammar school children to Cornwall. Then came the Labour Government's push for comprehensive education, a principle adopted by the islands' Education Committee. There was a referendum, public meetings, and much fury. Some parents wanted the fuller opportunities offered by the bigger schools in Cornwall; loyal islanders feared that children educated there would never settle in the islands again.

The new school had been started as a secondary modern in 1965, across the road from Carn Thomas. In 1966 the full Council of the Isles voted for comprehensive education, and the new building was opened as a comprehensive school in September 1968. With ten teachers and eighty pupils it was the smallest comprehensive in Britain. Off-island children board during the week and go home at weekends. Sixth-formers are boarded on the mainland. In 1972, of the first group of eighteen children who had received all their secondary education at the new school, fourteen had General Certificate of Education passes and all had CSE passes. Thirteen were going on to further education on the mainland.

But by 1972 the intake of the St Mary's schools was double that estimated ten years before. The council, after more battles, resolved to improve and extend the existing schools, and build a second primary school. The comprehensive school had cost £140,000; now the estimated bill was £250,000. The unthinkable alternative was to cease being a local education authority. On the off-islands the problem was reversed; by 1964 the school population had fallen to twenty-eight on Tresco, fifteen on St Martin's, seven on Bryher and five on Agnes. A new schoolmaster on Bryher brought three children of his own, but when he left in 1972 the school had to close. The few children are taken to Tresco each day but the building is kept in repair and there are hopes that the school population of Bryher may grow enough to open the school again. Agnes was down to two children of school age in 1973 but daily transport from that more isolated island was out of the question and the school remained open.

When the late Mr A. G. A. McMillan Browse became headmaster of Carn Thomas School in 1949 he revived the old school picnic on Samson, where for many inter-war years all the island schools had met in a joint revel. He started school visits to the mainland and found that many of his pupils not only had never been to the mainland, but they had never visited an island other than their own. The tours extended into Europe and farther afield; when Mr Browse retired in 1968 some of his pupils made a school trip to the Holy Land for Christmas; one young Scillonian sophisticate reported that he 'found Bethlehem trippery'.

12 THE PEOPLE AND THEIR ORIGINS

WHO are the Scillonians; where did they come from? The turbulent medieval history of the islands suggests that they were depopulated, or reduced to a handful of people, more than once, the inhabitants fleeing from pirates, outlaws and raiders, or being slaughtered by them. There was a long period of lawlessness in English home waters during the Wars of the Roses, and then as naval strength built up the pirates retreated to remote places like Scilly. Almost a century of such conditions culminated in the Seymour purchase, when Scilly was 'a bushment of briars and a refuge for all the pirates that ranged'. That century seems to have depopulated the islands altogether, and not until the 1540–60 fortifications were built on St Mary's and Tresco did people move back into their shelter. Godolphin reported to Queen Elizabeth in 1579 that only the two defended islands, St Mary's and Tresco, were inhabited. Since the islands had come into his possession (in 1570), eighty tenements had been erected, and 'laborious inclosures of rough ground' made. There were not 100 men but more women and children, which would be about the population of eighty tenements.

There may have been survivors from earlier times but 'the bushment of briars', the 'laborious inclosure of rough ground', both suggest a new start. Place names are little help. Latin references to the Silurian islands and *Sylinam insulam* may or may not refer to Scilly. The final 'y' may be the Norse word for island, with Viking links. Not until the charter of AD 927 which refers to Athelstan taking possession of *Sillanes insulae* are we on certain ground. The first English spelling is 'Sullye' in Henry I's time and 'Sully', 'Silly' or Sylly' continue in general use until the seventeenth century when the 'c' seems to have been inserted to defeat the jokers. For that reason the official name today is 'the Isles of Scilly'. Leland who wrote about 1540 used 'Scylley' but his account did not appear in print until 1710. 'Scillonian' as an adjective first appeared in a verse by Robert Heath in 1744.

There are Celtic names like Rosevear and Rosevean, but they could be Cornish, Welsh or Breton, and not of great antiquity. Godolphin could be expected to bring in tenants from his Cornish estates and villages, who would bring their home names with them. Borlase gave the names of the St Mary's farms in 1752; most were named after their occupiers, like Bant's tenement. There are only two Cornish place names, Trenowith, a west Cornish form of Trenouth which simply means 'new farm', and Helvear.

If from place names one turns to family names, the parish registers of St Mary's, which begin in 1726, are the natural starting place. By 1740 only four Cornish surnames appear, Tregarthen, Treweek, Trenear and Pender. The researches of Richard Blewett suggests that the Tregarthens came from Ludgvan, the Treweeks from Stithians, the Trenears from Madron and the Penders from St Buryan. All are villages in west Cornwall, in the Godolphin area of influence. There are even traces of true Godolphin blood in the islands. The seventh child of Francis, the first leaseholder of 1570, was his daughter Ursula, who married her father's agent in the islands, John Crudge of Holy Vale. Their younger son William settled at Holy Vale after his parents, and the family continued in St Mary's for nearly 200 years. But by the time the Crudge name died out various daughters had married into the MacFarlane, Mumford, Banfield and Tregarthen families. These families survived into modern times, and many Scillonians must be descended from Ursula Godolphin.

But just as the bulk of the early farm names are of English origin, so are the surnames found in the first Scilly parish register: Mumford, Watts, Stideford, Hooper and Hicks. The last two names could be of Cornish origin. If it is reasonable to expect Francis Godolphin to find Cornish tenants for his Scilly farms, it must be realised that his family had imported Germans to improve their Cornish tin mines a few years earlier, and would not have been above finding Englishmen for Scilly. To the end of Elizabeth's time he was finding soldiers to man the Scilly garrison; he had to look beyond Cornwall for them as likely as not. Garrison troops have always left their mark on the islands.

Borlase, writing of his 1752 visit (in which he says that the Godolphins 'brought here such a number of people, that all notice of the old Inhabitants was soon lost'), says in his manuscript that after the Civil War many of the Royalists stayed on to wait for better times: 'I conclude that from this great resort in the Civil Wars, and soon after, the greatest part of the present inhabitants are derived.' This is supposed to explain why the islanders (to quote Borlase again) 'are comely, civil to strangers and remarkable for speaking good English'. Certainly there is little Cornish accent in the islands. Baring Gould, an unreliable historian, has a story that after the Civil War a Bedfordshire regiment sent to the islands was forgotten, that the men married locally and settled down. It is hard to think of even the least competent régimes at the War Office losing a whole regiment! There is a legend in the Edwards family that their ancestors came from Shropshire about 1650, fleeing from Cromwellian persecution, and that the Mumfords and Banfields came at the same time. They were all said to be farmers and the Edwards settled at Trenoweth, the Banfields at Holy Vale and the Mumfords at Longstone; further, none of them were ever noted as boatmen, save for some master mariner Mumfords.

Staying with the military origins of families, the McFarlands and McDonalds are said to have been soldiers of a Scottish regiment who settled. Count Magalotti's record of 1669 says that the 200-strong garrison had been forbidden to marry local girls because corn was getting scarce, so clearly it had been happening. Some men of the Companies of Invalids married and settled and old men are not beyond founding families. Some of the workmen employed on the nineteenth-century fortifications married and stayed. So did some of the soldiers who manned the guns at the turn of the century; the widow of one died as recently as 1966.

The first Wood settled from the 1914–18 naval base. Land Army girls in the 1939–45 war stayed on as island wives. D. H. Rogers, a pilot who plunged to the bottom of Crow Sound in his Hurricane, married Nancy Stideford of Lunnon and farms there now. The soldier who settles is as old as history.

Every port in the world has had its visiting sailors who stayed on, usually because they had got their knees under a comfortable table. Captain Reseigh of *Scillonian* fame first came to the islands in 1910 as a cook in a coaster looking for salvage work at the wreck of the *Minnehaha*. Apart from sailors there have been coastguards, preventive men, lighthouse keepers and builders. The Watts families on St Mary's have a common Great-Grandfather Bastian who was a preventive officer from St Keverne in Cornwall. Amos Clarke of Rotherhithe, the 1720s lighthouse keeper on Agnes, married into the Hicks family and the Clarke name is not forgotten. Tiddy the gig builder came from St Mawes (he probably learnt his trade with the Peters) and married Anne Dowling of Scilly, whose forebears came from Ulster. Teffin Richardson who died aged ninety-two in 1949 was a Bishop Rock workman in 1882 who married and settled.

John Grenfell Moyle arrived as the island doctor in 1849, married a local girl and worked in the islands for forty-one years. His son married a niece of William Trevellick, the flower pioneer of Rocky Hill, and became a power in the islands. Vic Treneary, a taxi driver, was the grandson of a noted hedger of Sennen whom Augustus Smith brought over to work on the developing estate. The renowned W. N. 'Fuzzy' Groves reached Penzance after World War II looking for work; he jumped on the steamer out of impulse and became, in all his activities, an island 'character'.

But just as soldiers in garrison or visiting seamen have settled in Scilly, so Scillonian seamen have settled in all corners of the world where a good job or a pretty girl took their eye. There has been a two-way traffic into Scilly and out of it as long as records give any evidence. When those first west Cornish settlers were getting their name into the parish registers of St Mary's, one can find bridegrooms in many west Cornish parishes described as 'of

Scilly'. Some of the later emigrants can be traced: Richard Trevellick of St Mary's was born in 1835, became a shipyard apprentice, travelled the world before settling in Detroit where he
fought for equal rights for all men and women, was instrumental
in founding the National Labor Union in 1866, and is still remembered in Labor Day, the public holiday now accepted as the
last day of the summer vacation season in the United States. His
nephew William Trevellick Edwards fittingly started in the
flower trade on Vancouver Island. Another emigrant, John
Deason of Tresco, was working in the Australian goldfields in
1869 when he put his pick into the biggest nugget ever found,
weighing 2,268oz. A monument marks the spot in central Victoria, and there are still Deasons on St Mary's.

In spite of the movement of people, in and out of the islands,
some names have persisted. Apart from the parish registers, early
wills are a source of information. In the period 1704–1851 the
common names are Nicholas, Nicholls, Pender, Watts, Nance,
Phillips, Tregarthen, Ellis, Sherris, Edwards, Gibson, Mumford,
Hooper, Jenkin and Stideford. In 1823 Woodley recorded the
common names of the islands: Jenkins 40 families, Ellis 35, Hicks
30, Pender 27, Woodcock 25, Odger 20, Ashford 17, Webber 12
and Gibson 8.

The population table on p 188 shows the total population of
the islands growing slowly from the Elizabethan reoccupation to
the outbreak of the Revolutionary and Napoleonic Wars, adding
about 500 people in both the seventeenth and eighteenth centuries. Then, with the prosperity brought by those wars, comes a
jump of 1,000 people in thirty years with a peak of 2,616 inhabitants in 1821 which, allowing for men away at sea, remains fairly
steady until 1851. In spite of all the stories of Augustus Smith's
deportations there is no great fall-off in the first twenty years of
his régime. After 1851 there is a general fall right up to World
War II. Since then population has risen again, back in general
terms to the level of a century ago.

Half the population of the islands has always been on St
Mary's, but as the years have passed so the proportion has become greater. In fact it is clear that though the 1790–1820 in-

Population of the Isles of Scilly

Date	Total	St Mary's	Tresco	Agnes	St Martin's	Bryher	Samson	Tean	St Helen's	Notes and sources
1551	c250	300	✓	✓	✓	✓	✓	✓	✓	Commission to Sir W. Godolphin
1579	c300	300	✓	✓	✓	✓	✓	✓	✓	Godolphin report
1669	c1,000	✓	✓	✓	✓	✓	✓	✓	✓	Grand Duke Cosmo. Only 1 family on Samson, 1 on St Helen's
1715	822	477	139	66	64	54	12	10	—	Colonel Lilley
1744	1,400	c700	✓	✓	✓	✓	✓	?	—	Heath
1790	1,430	650	350	185	170	60	15	?	—	Molly Mortimer
1801	2,465									Victoria County History of Cornwall
1808	2,120	1,165	411	215	206	90	33	—	—	Royal Cornwall Gazette
1821	2,616	1,400	480	282	280	140	34	—	—	Victoria County History of Cornwall
1831	2,465	1,311	470	289	230	128	37	—	—	Victoria County History of Cornwall
1841	2,582	1,545	430	243	214	121	29	—	—	Census. About 215 islanders away at sea
1851	2,627	1,668	416	204	211	118	10	—	—	Census
1861	2,431	1,532	399	200	185	115	—	—	—	Census. 37 seamen, not islanders, included
1871	2,117	1,383	266	179	185	104	—	—	—	Census. 15 seamen, not islanders, included
1881	2,320	1,566	325	151	175	103	—	—	—	Census. 276 seamen, not islanders, included
1891	1,911	1,201	315	130	174	91	—	—	—	Census
1901	2,092	1,355	331	134	175	97	—	—	—	Census
1911	2,097	1,376	315	102	191	113	—	—	—	Census
1921	1,749	1,196	217	101	134	101	—	—	—	Census. Greatest decrease in UK
1931	1,740	1,216	248	78	134	64	—	—	—	Census
1941										No census
1951	2,194	1,625	243	78	131	117	—	—	—	Census
1961	2,288	1,736	283	85	118	66	—	—	—	Census
1970	est 2,000		190	60	95	45	—	—	—	SW Econ Planning Committee Report est
1971	2,430	1,958	246	63	106	57	—	—	—	Census, including 290 hotel guests
1973	2,040	1,650	180	65	90	55	—	—	—	Estimate of June residents; visitors omitted

General note: Census figures include visitors. Estimates only cover residents crease was shared by all the islands, the post-1945 increase is almost entirely confined to St Mary's.

Godolphin's reoccupation was limited to the two fortified islands but in the following century there was an outward colonisation. Count Magalotti was in St Mary's in March 1669; his figures are based on hearsay but he reports a total population of about 1,000 with seven islands occupied, though Samson and St Helen's each had only one family. Bryher and Agnes seem to have been continuously occupied since that date. Woodley says that in 1821 a quarter of the people on Tresco and a third on Bryher were named Jenkins. That is still true of Bryher, but on Tresco there has been a considerable move in and out of families and though old Scilly names survive they by no means dominate. There have always been links between Bryher and Tresco because of their closeness, but Bryher men have always been considered in the islands as a stolid race.

The Jenkins name comes in the early parish registers and Mrs Honiton (herself of Jenkin descent) says the name was first spelt Jenkyn and she describes them as a clan on Tresco and Bryher, 'squatters, asserting themselves, paying attention neither to Godolphin nor Leeds, swaggering around Tresco island, owning the earth, disregarding the law'. They were often in trouble with authority and opposed Augustus Smith. Is this a wild Welsh strain which had fled from trouble they had made for themselves in Wales?

In spite of Count Magalotti it is generally held that St Martin's was reoccupied in the 1680s when Mr Ekins was the Godolphin steward. He is believed to have installed four families there, the Ellis, Babbs, Woodcock and Ashford clans. The Nance family which moved into Tean at about this time to burn kelp moved to St Martin's soon afterwards and it was the Nances who built the Signal Row farm. Nance blood survives in the Stevens family, and there are still Ashfords, but a quarter of the islanders now are Goddards, though the name does not appear in an 1851 directory. St Martin's like all the islands has suffered from emigration; the Gibson family of photographers in Hugh Town came originally from St Martin's where the name appears in the first parish register of 1727. There was also a major move out of St Martin's at the end of the Dorrien Smith lease in 1922 when forty people declined the Duchy terms and moved to the mainland. But islanders say you can still recognise a man from St Martin's by his fair hair and blue eyes; the old nickname for them is 'Ginnick'. Until the modern gig-racing fever caught them they tended to stand aloof from the people of the other islands and a group of St Martin's men do look a race apart.

Agnes, the other remote island, is the home of the Hickses; Woodley said that half the islanders had this name but today they are only a third. They are a dark, swarthy clan, nicknamed 'Turks', and Whitfield in 1852 called them 'a true Celtic race, masculine, untidy, litigious, given to fun, strong liquor and scandal, wielding a hoe for potatoes with one hand and brandishing a blackthorn in the other'. They were the great pilotage family but as piloting failed they had to move out. Two celebrated Tresco characters, Obadiah Hicks and Willy Howard Jenkins were both born on Agnes. But the story of Mrs Wain Smith, schoolmistress on Agnes from 1941 to 1952, illustrates what happens even in these lonely communities. Her son settled on the island and three of her daughters married island men, and when she died in 1968 four of the fifteen married couples on the island were of her family.

Samson in its days of occupation had only two families, Webber and Woodcock. They had a lively history. Mrs Honiton relates that the Webbers and the Woodcocks, who first lived on and around Sandy Bay on St Mary's, were of unknown origin but by some said to be descended from wrecked privateersmen. They had a long feud with the Banfields and the Mumfords, who ran things for the Godolphins, and eventually the Council of Twelve sent the military to arrest Liquer Webber and his family, and Dicebox Woodcock and his, as being dangers to the community. They were ordered to live in various batteries about the islands and serve in their defence. But Liquer and Dicebox would have none of this; they slipped off to Samson and established themselves there. The families were badly hit when nineteen of their men were lost in the French privateer they captured in 1801 and the surviving women largely married into other islands.

Augustus Smith finally moved the surviving families off Samson in 1855. The daughter of a woman who at twelve years of age was one of the children evacuated by Smith from Samson married James Thomas Lethbridge, a Plymouth man who, after serving at sea in square-rigged ships, came to Scilly to work on Bishop Rock. He was forty years in the St Mary's lifeboat, for a time served as second cox and had four sons in the crew, all of course of Samson descent. The Woodcocks are still in Scilly, respectable and esteemed, but the Webber name has disappeared.

So not only on St Mary's and Tresco, but on the other islands too, though the old names and the old blood survive, new blood and new names are constantly coming in. It is the story of the islands; even the old blood is not so very old if one takes the standard of remote rural areas in other parts of England. The editor of the *Scillonian* wrote in 1972, 'Not many real Scillonians now – maybe 80 to 100.' Probably what is true today has always been true; there are natives of Scilly scattered right across the globe, and new people moving into the islands to take their place. A check through the Bryher voters' list of 1967 was revealing. Of the forty-one people of voting age only twenty-two were natives, and of those eight were of retirement age. One would probably find on all the islands that half the people were not natives, and the constant influx of new blood may be all to the good. The people are generally reputed to be more friendly than those in Devon and Cornwall; less inhibited and certainly without class consciousness. Those who leave the islands are always anxious to talk about them, to make return visits and to see islanders when they visit the mainland. But those who leave rarely return to live in Scilly. The converse is true. Older people who retire to the islands often move out again as they get less able to look after themselves, but the young who move in and stay over a year or two rarely get away. They become assimilated.

13   WILD LIFE

THE isolation of Scilly, and the position of the islands in the Atlantic west of the main land mass, means many variations from the British norm in the wild life of Scilly. Isolation commonly reduces the number of species found in any category, and this is particularly marked in land mammals. There are no foxes, badgers, hedgehogs, stoats, weasels, hares or moles; on the other hand there are white-toothed shrews unknown elsewhere in Britain, though allied to a sub-species in Brittany. The Scilly shrew is named after the islands, *Crocidura suaveolens cassiteridum*. Rabbits, a Norman introduction to England, were recorded in the islands in 1176. Augustus Smith tried stocking different islands with different colours, and they are said to be predominantly black on Samson, white on St Helen's and dun-coloured on St Mary's. Smith also tried to make Samson into a deer park but the animals are long gone.

Birdlife reflects the same island limitations. Among landbirds there are no hawks except kestrels, no owls, ravens, crows, jackdaws or magpies, no woodpeckers, nuthatches or treecreepers. The absence of woods for many centuries (there is evidence of trees in prehistoric times) explains the lack of woodland birds, but since Tresco has become wooded in the past century so the great tit and blue tit have arrived. Some of the predators and crows are seen occasionally but their general absence is thought to account for the birds on the islands, particularly Tresco, seeming remarkably tame; they have no natural enemies. Skylarks, wrens, thrushes, blackbirds and sparrows are common.

Freshwater birds abound on the islands and waterfowl, apart from geese, range from swans to the tiny teal. Of the waders, the ringed plover and the oyster-catcher breed and there are varied visitors for most months of the year. But seabirds provide the great riches. Shags, cormorants, great black-backed gulls and herring gulls are resident. Lesser black-backed gulls and kittiwakes come early to breed. Guillemots, razorbills, puffins, Manx shearwaters and storm petrels begin to arrive at the end of March, followed by fulmars.

A bird observatory was set up on Agnes in 1957; by 1965 it had ringed birds of 121 species. Since 1957 Annet and most uninhabited islands and rocks have been closed to visitors during the three months of the breeding season, and further restrictions were imposed after the *Torrey Canyon* disaster cut heavily into seabird numbers. More restrictions came in 1970 because so many birdwatchers were visiting islands. All but the inhabited islands are under the guardianship of the Nature Conservancy with their lessee, Mr Dorrien Smith, and Mr P. Z. Mackenzie their wardens. The local committee of the Nature Conservancy has at least two observers on each island. A St Mary's ornithologist, David Hunt, has organised successful wild-life holidays since the early 1970s.

Probably the parrot-like puffin most attracts the visitor, though their numbers are inexplicably reduced in modern times. They can still be seen on Annet, Men-a-vawr, St Helen's and the outer isles. But Scilly's importance in ornithology lies in its rarities, which most birdwatchers come to look for. Apart from colourful birds like the hoopoe and golden oriole, which can more likely be seen in the islands than anywhere else in Britain, there are prime rarities reported regularly from the Arctic, north Africa and even north America. Indeed the islands since 1970 have had a special annual migration record published, and October 1971 was exciting enough with its rarities to merit a special article in *British Birds*. There has been a long dispute as to how some of the smaller American landbirds cross so wide a stretch of ocean, but there is a theory that, apart from the obvious help of the prevailing westerly wind, they rest on eastbound ships while on passage.

Reptiles show the island limitations too; there are frogs on St Mary's but on none of the other islands; the whole group is without toads or snakes. The numbers of species of spiders have

M

been shown to vary according to the size of each island's land mass, ranging from ninety-one on St Mary's to none on the smallest rocks, but fewer than on the adjacent mainland. Beetles show similar limitations, although some have not been found in England but are believed to originate from much more southerly Atlantic coasts. Butterflies have been studied for island variations developed in isolation; the Meadow Brown on Tean has anything from none to five spots on the wing while those found in Devon and Cornwall have none or two. St Helen's, $\frac{1}{2}$ mile away, has produced a different variation. Butterflies from North America, notably the Monarch, have also been observed.

The sea shore is a happy hunting ground for the marine biologist because of the great variation in coast, from storm-battered rocks to sheltered fine sands, in a small compass. Again some species common on the mainland, like the periwinkle and the common mussel, are rare, while there are a small number of a great variety which are common in the Mediterranean and the north African shores. For visitors the most exciting marine mammals are the grey seals which breed in the Western Rocks and the Eastern Islands. The bulls reach up to $8\frac{1}{2}$ft in length but the all-white pups attract most attention, lying on the rocks. Basking sharks up to 40ft in length can be seen in summer months on the crossing from Penzance and the smaller Atlantic sharks are not uncommon. Dolphins and porpoises can be seen, other species of whales are not unknown, and even turtles have been reported, from warmer waters. Constant westerly winds can also bring in other marine life rare in this country, notably the Portuguese Man-o'-War which the layman sees as a large purple jellyfish. Over ninety varieties of fish have been identified round the islands.

The islands' flora is limited like everything else by the island isolation but the limited species flourish in the moist warm air. The winter freedom from frost encourages vegetation not hardy in England and there are a number of species found in Scilly that have spread up from the Mediterranean. The untrained visitor will appreciate the gold and purple carpet of heather and little gorse on the downs in autumn, the garlic growing like white bluebells through all the lanes of St Mary's in spring, the strange fleshy mesembryanthemums running wild and the climbing geraniums covering cottage fronts. For the botanist there are endless pleasures, chiefly in comparing the vegetation of small islands that have either never or only briefly been inhabited, in seeing how garden plants have in places run wild, and in seeing how all vegetation adapts to the unusual climate with its contrasts of exposure.

IN 1964 the Council of the Isles invited Geoffrey Jellicoe, a member of the Fine Art Commission and a prominent architect and planner, to draw up a landscape charter for the islands. Published in 1965, this contained three basic articles. The first suggested retaining and defending the status quo of the landscape, and to this end limiting both internal development and the influx of visitors. The second suggested a landing charge on all visitors to the islands, the proceeds to maintain agriculture and the landscape. The third, administrative, suggested a joint consultative committee of the Council of the Isles and the Duchy. The whole, it was suggested, should be the basis of a charter for the islands which the council, as the planning authority, and the Duchy, as the freeholder outside Hugh Town, should support.

Mr Jellicoe regarded the bulb industry as almost fully developed but the tourist industry underdeveloped, though such development might 'trample out or chase away the very things by which it was created'. St Mary's, though romantic, he saw as just a detached fragment of the mainland, a stepping-stone to the off-islands. 'For these a primitive character must be maintained without the imposition of a primitive existence.'

He saw St Mary's continuing on a complex mainland economy, and recommended that development be limited to Hugh Town, Old Town and Porthloo, trees to screen the visually damaging houses on McFarland's Down, and a single camp site limited to 120 on a single field south of Star Castle. Tresco he saw continuing as self-supporting on its dual economy of farming and tourism. Bryher, Agnes and St Martin's he expected to continue dependent on farming, and urged that their populations should be kept stable, that the Duchy should supply better amenities for residents and that no additional holiday accommodation should be allowed.

In the islands there were divided views about the landing charge, though it was obvious that the practice, already adopted on Tresco, was working to that island's advantage. But there was a general feeling that some development should be allowed in the off-islands, and strong criticism was forthcoming. Ewart Johns, a lecturer in geography at Exeter University and a regular visitor to Agnes, wrote that the Jellicoe Report would make St Mary's another South Coast resort, and the off-islands a native reserve, a sort of zoo with gawpers walking tidy paths between the flower fields. Off-islanders had already been saying much the same thing.

The South West Economic Planning Committee was also at work on an economic survey, though it did not appear till April 1971. Their planners estimated the income from flowers at £175,000 and from tourism at £700,000 a year. Not only did they rate tourism as four times as profitable as flowers, but visualised a 2 per cent growth for tourism and none for flowers. Like Jellicoe they proposed a strict limit on housing development, but they opposed any landing charge and suggested that money proposed for St Mary's road improvements would be better spent on the inter-island launch service.

When the report came to future policy for the off-islands, it ran into trouble. Because of depopulation, lack of some essential services, heavy dependence on the flower industry and little diversification into tourism, the report could see their future imperilled. With regret it suggested that council policy should concentrate on maintaining the population of the two most viable off-islands, Tresco and St Martin's. Bryher was described as being economically the weakest. But the Council of the Isles rejected this policy and, when in June 1972 a financial survey of the islands showed that the off-islands only contributed 10·9 per cent of the rate income but had 21·5 per cent spent on them, it came under sharp attack. How much the off-islands benefited the economy of St Mary's, it was argued in defence, would only be found out if the off-islands were depopulated.

But the council did accept the control of development advocated by both Jellicoe and the Economic Planning Council. At their meeting in February 1973 a ban was placed on all future housing development on St Mary's, apart from proposals in the pipeline, and all conversion of large houses into flats was to be discouraged. They would only provide houses in future for necessary workers, retired workers and other 'qualifying people'. The Duchy also planned to introduce the landing charge, advocated by the Jellicoe Report, for every visitor to Scilly. Strong opposition developed in the Council of the Isles, but the idea was 'accepted in principle' by the council in May 1973. For the off-islands the Duchy, even when faced with the closure of Bryher School for lack of pupils, declared that they did not accept that any of the off-islands should be allowed to run down naturally, but favoured modest development on Bryher, Agnes and St Martin's. In recent years the Duchy has been steadily improving living standards on these three islands; one might reasonably accept that in spite of census figures the off-islands will continue inhabited.

All the islands will change, inevitably, as they have changed throughout their history. As communications improve, so the way of life comes more into the mainstream of English life. But the two industries of tourism and flower growing are complementary; they make their labour demands at different times of the year and indeed most resorts would be glad of a second industry like the flowers of Scilly to give winter employment. Hugh Town in particular will more and more resemble a South Coast resort. Duchy policy and the development of farming will make St Mary's outside Hugh Town a place of bigger farms working closer together. On Tresco the late Commander Dorrien Smith set a pattern for the other off-islands and in his short sojourn in the council chair he was getting his ideas more generally accepted. Running that island as a combined farming-holiday unit clearly works.

On St Martin's the Duchy policy of building bigger, more economic farm units is finding expression through Mr Dallimore. In such small communities this kind of development can only be slow, but one would expect this to happen in due course on Bryher and Agnes. Some of Tresco's growing prosperity is rubbing off on Bryher, and the strong community spirit of the Agnes 'Turks', and its wildness, will always be an asset.

The one great threat to life on Scilly as it is now is might be the finding of gas or oil fields under the seabed close by. By 1974 Shell was licensed to explore five areas 50 miles west of the islands, and an even larger area of exploration had been licensed, beginning 50 miles north. BP planned to drill six exploratory wells in this area in 1974. The major defence of Scilly against the islands becoming a base for oil rigs or their crews is the shallowness of the harbours. An additional defence came in 1973 with the proposed designation of the islands by the Countryside Commission as an area of outstanding natural beauty. Apart from requiring higher standards in any development, this designation also provides Whitehall grants for the enhancing of amenities.

In the middle 1960s it looked as if Duchy neglect of the off-islands, an apparent policy of treating all the islands as a business concern, only spending money if a reasonable return on capital could be expected, might be disastrous. No change of heart has been publicly expressed but it seems to have come about. Once before in history the off-islands were left to fend for themselves and it brought the distresses of the 1820s. Now it is realised that though Scilly has five inhabited islands it is one community, indivisible. St Mary's tourist prosperity can be seen in the crowds which take the launches every morning of the season to the off-islands; the tourists spend little more than their fares but they would not be spending their money on St Mary's either if the off-islands were not there to visit, or if Hugh Town was all.

Butlin was turned away from Samson. A sensible limitation on the number of visitors, a sharp control of all development, a determination to see that even the most remote inhabitant can enjoy the basic amenities of modern life, and a strong and constant concern for the natural beauty of Scilly, seems to be the policy that both Duchy and council are pursuing. It seems to be right.

Life is not easy on these lonely islands. But it would be hard to destroy their character, born of the hard life and the sea, and hard to damage their incomparable beauty. Their peace could only be destroyed by monumental folly, and the people of the islands are not fools. They value their way of life and the setting in which it is passed. On the off-islands one can almost hear the sigh of relief when the last boat has left for St Mary's in the afternoon, but one suspects too that the people welcome the visitors for 'a bit of company'. And they are not afraid of hard work. As my old friend Len Jenkins, the boatman of Bryher, once said when we were debating his island's future, 'If you put your shoulder to the wheel, the wheel will turn.'

BIBLIOGRAPHY

M Y basic source for this book was a complete set of *Scillonian* magazines, an invaluable record not only for the steady reporting but for the innumerable articles on the history of the islands. The detailed references to the *Scillonian*, and to all the printed works consulted, are lodged with a second copy of the full typescript with the Museum of the Isles of Scilly. Four books are the mainstay of everyone who studies Scilly, and to them I would add two modern works. These six are, in chronological order:

HEATH, ROBERT. *A Natural and Historical Account of the Islands of Scilly* (1750)

BORLASE, WILLIAM. *Observations on the Ancient and Present State of the Islands of Scilly* (1756)

TROUTBECK, JOHN. *A Survey of the Ancient and Present State of the Scilly Islands* (c1796)

WOODLEY, GEORGE. *A View of the Present State of the Scilly Islands* (1822)

GRIGSON, GEOFFREY. *The Scilly Isles* (1948)

MATTHEWS, G. FORRESTER. *The Isles of Scilly* (1960)

Grigson I have long used as a guide though its format fits no pocket; Matthews is invaluable as a study of the constitutional, economic and social life of the islands. Other sources consulted in the preparation of this book are:

ALDRIDGE, JESSIE. *Hobnails and Sea-boots* (1956)

ARLOTT, JOHN, *et al. Island Camera: The Isles of Scilly in the Photography of the Gibson Family* (1973)

BLEWITT, RICHARD. 'Researches into Cornish Families', *Western Morning News* (17 August 1965; 14, 21 and 24 May 1968)

BOWEN, FRANK. *H.M. Coastguards* (1928)

BOWLEY, E. L. *The Fortunate Islands* (4th ed, 1957)

CARSON, EDWARD. *The Ancient & Rightful Customs* (1972)

CHADWICK, NORA K. *Celtic Britain* (1963)

BIBLIOGRAPHY

CHOPE, R. PEARSE (ed). *Early Tours in Devon & Cornwall* (1918; new ed, 1967)

CHRISTOPHER, KENNETH. Article in *Agriculture*, No 70 (1964)

CLEIFE, PHILIP. *Airway to the Isles* (1966)

COATE, MARY. *Cornwall in the Great Civil War* (1933)

DOBLE, CANON GILBERT H. *Saints of Cornwall* (1964)

DORRIEN SMITH, CHARLOTTE. *Shipwrecks of the Isles of Scilly* (1953)

DOUCH, H. C. *Cornish Windmills* (1963)

DUDLEY, DOROTHY and BUTCHER, SARNIA. *Nornour*, Isles of Scilly Museum Pub No 7 (revised ed, 1970)

DUNBAR, JOHN. *The Lost Land: Underwater Exploration in the Isles of Scilly* (1958)

ELKINS, P. J. 'Postal Affairs of the Isles of Scilly', *Stamp Collecting* (24 July 1964)

ELLIOTT-BINNS, L. E. *Medieval Cornwall* (1955)

FARR, GRAHAME. *West Country Passenger Steamers* (1967)

FINBERG, H. P. R. *Tavistock Abbey* (1951)

FLETCHER, CANON J. R. *Short History of St Michael's Mount* (1951)

GIBSON, ALEXANDER. *Isles of Scilly: Visitor's Companion in Sunny Lyonnesse* (1932)

GILLIS, R. H. C. 'Pilot Gigs of Cornwall & the Isles of Scilly', *Journal, Royal Institution of Cornwall*, Vol V, Pt 2 (1966)

Guide to Tresco Abbey Gardens

HALL, P. L. *The Caption of Seisin of the Duchy of Cornwall, 1337* (Devon & Cornwall Record Society, 1971)

HUNT, LESLIE. 'Scilly and the Royal Air Force', *Western Morning News* (25 October 1968)

INGLIS-JONES, E. *Augustus Smith of Scilly* (1969)

LARN, RICHARD. *Cornish Shipwrecks*, Vol 3, *The Isles of Scilly* (1971)

LELAND, JOHN. *The Itinerary*, ed Smith, L. T. (1907)

LOUSLEY, J. E. *The Flora of the Isles of Scilly* (1971)

LYONS, DAVID and SAMUEL. *Magna Britannia*, Vol III (Cornwall) (1814)

McDONALD, KENDALL. *The Wreck Detectors* (1972)

MARCH, E. J. *Inshore Craft of Britain in Days of Sail & Oar* (1970)

MARSHALL, BEATRICE (ed) *Memoirs of Lady Fanshawe* (1676)

MAYBEE, ROBERT. *Sixty-Eight Years Experience on the Scilly Isles*, Isles of Scilly Museum Publication No 9 (1973)

MORRIS, ROLAND. *Island Treasure* (1969)

MOTHERSOLE, JESSIE. *Isles of Scilly* (1910)

MUMFORD, CLIVE. *Portrait of the Isles of Scilly* (1967)

NOALL, CYRIL and FARR, GRAHAME. *Wreck & Rescue Round the Cornish Coast*, Vol II, *The Story of the Land's End Lifeboats* (1965)

NOALL, CYRIL. *History of Cornish Stage Coaches* (1963)

——. *Cornish Lights & Shipwrecks* (1968)

OLIVER, GEORGE, DD. *Monasticon Diocesis Exoniensis* (1846)

O'NEIL. *Ancient Monuments of Isles of Scilly* (2nd ed, 1961; amended ed, 1971)

O'NEILL, MRS H. E. 'Excavation of a Celtic Hermitage on St Helen's, Isles of Scilly', *Archaeological Journal*, Vol CXXI (1964)

PICKWELL, JOHN. *Shipwrecks around the Isles of Scilly*, Isles of Scilly Museum Publication No 3 (1967)

POWELL, A. C. 'Glass Making in Bristol', *Trans Bristol & Gloucestershire Arch Society*, Vol XVII (1925)

QUICK, H. M. *Birds of the Scilly Isles* (1964)

QUIXLEY, R. C. E. *Antique Maps of Cornwall & the Isles of Scilly* (1966)

ROCHE, T. W. L. *The King of Almayne* (1966)

ROGERS, BOB. *Excavation of H.M.S. Association* (nd)

ROWSE, A. L. *Tudor Cornwall* (1941)

——. *Cornish in America* (1969)

Royal Agricultural Society of England Journal, Vol VI, second series, Pt II, No 12 (1870)

SHAW, THOMAS. *History of Cornish Methodism* (1967)

SMITH, REV GEORGE. *Report detailing the Extreme Miseries of the Off-Islands of Scilly* (1818)

TANGYE, MICHAEL. *Scilly 1801–1821* (1970)

TONKIN, J. C. and R. W. *Guide to the Isles of Scilly* (1882)

TORR, CECIL. *Small Talk at Wreyland* (1918)

TURK, STELLA M. *Seashore Life in Cornwall and the Isles of Scilly* (1971)

Victoria County History of Cornwall (1906)

VYVYAN, C. G. *The Scilly Isles* (1953)

INDEX

Page numbers in italic indicate illustrations